Ultimate Restaurant Design

teNeues

Ultimate Restaurant Design

Editor in chief: Paco Asensio

Project coordination and texts: Ana Cristina G. Cañizares, Aurora Cuito

Art director: Mireia Casanovas Soley

Layout: J. L. Crespo

Copy editing: Susana González

Editorial assistant: Marta Casado

German translation: Anette Hilgendag

French translation: Marion Westerhoff

Italian translation: Sara Tonelli

Published by teNeues Publishing Group

teNeues Publishing Company
16 West 22nd Street
New York, NY 10010, USA
Tel.: 001-212-627-9090, Fax: 001-212-627-9511

teNeues Book Division
Kaistraße 18
40221 Düsseldorf, Germany
Tel.: 0049-(0)211-99 45 97-0, Fax: 0049-(0)211-99 45 97-40

teNeues Publishing UK Ltd.
P.O. Box 402
West Byfleet
KT14 7ZF, Great Britain
Tel.: 0044-1932-403509, Fax: 0044-1932-403514

teNeues France S.A.R.L.
4, rue de Valence
75005 Paris, France
Tel: 0033-1-55 76-62 05, Fax: 0033-1-55 76-64 19

www.teneues.com

ISBN: 3-8238-4595-0

Editorial project: 2004 LOFT Publications
Via Laietana 32, 4º Of. 92
08003 Barcelona, Spain
Tel.: 0034 932 688 088
Fax: 0034 932 687 073

e-mail: loft@loftpublications.com
www.loftpublications.com

Printed by: Anman Gràfiques del Vallès, Spain
www.anman.com
2004

Bibliographic information published by
Die Deutsche Bibliothek.
Die Deutsche Bibliothek lists this publication
in the Deutsche Nationalbibliografie;
detailed bibliographic data is available
in the Internet at http://dnb.ddb.de

America

Australia
Asia

Europe

Within the large number of places that comprise the fabric of today's contemporary urban land-scape, public interior venues are taking on an ever-growing significance in the face of exterior spaces. Whether in terms of climate, security, leisure or well-being, interiors have naturally incor-porated themselves into the daily urban itinerary as a part of public activity.

The intense social interaction that takes place within these public spaces is concentrated within bars and restaurants, home to flirtations and friendships, entertainment and relaxation, observers and the observed. Over time, this type of establishment has taken on a singular and unique char-acter, straying away from the impersonal styles typical of past decades, and transforming them-selves into suggestive spaces that instigate a varied series of social relations.

The following pages illustrate a selection of bars and restaurants that communicate a particular attitude towards the wide range of sensations produced through the distinctive interior design of each environment. From the disquieting organic forms of the Georges, to the dramatic qualities of the Shu in Milan, an infinite number of solutions is reflected in each and every corner of these spaces. Thanks to the implementation of materials and the use of decorative objects, each estab-lishment engenders a series of conditions that determine in one way or another how people inter-act, and how to see and be seen.

Unsere heutige urbane Landschaft ist ein komplexes Gewebe aus Räumen und Plätzen unterschied-licher Gestalt. Dabei gewinnen öffentliche Interieurs gegenüber Plätzen im Freien immer mehr an Bedeutung. Öffentliche Interieurs sind aufgrund von Klimabedingungen, aus Sicherheitserwägungen oder bedingt durch die Anforderungen moderner Freizeitaktivitäten ein wesentlicher Teil der heutigen urbanen Architektur geworden.

Der intensive soziale Austausch, der in öffentlichen Räumen stattfindet, konzentriert sich in Bars und Restaurants: Orte für Flirts, einen Schwatz mit Freunden, Unterhaltung und Entspannung oder einfach ein Ort zum Sehen und Gesehenwerden. Diese Lokale haben mit der Zeit einen eigenen Charakter angenommen, der sich von dem unpersönlichen Stil unterscheidet, der sie noch vor wenigen Jahrzehnten auszeichnete. Bars und Restaurants sind zu interessanten Schauplätzen des modernen gesellschaftlichen Lebens geworden.

Die folgenden Seiten zeigen eine Reihe ausgewählter Bars und Restaurants, die durch ihr originel-les Innendesign hervorstechen und den Gast mit ihrem besonderen Ambiente gefangen nehmen. Von den organischen Formen des Georges bis zum radikalen Design des Mailänder Restaurants Shu werden die mannigfaltigen Details der hier vorgestellten Lokale den Betrachter immer wieder aufs Neue überraschen. Durch die verwendeten Materialien und die Anordnung der Dekorationsobjekte wurde in den einzelnen Lokalen ein jeweils einzigartiges Ambiente geschaffen, das den idealen Hintergrund für die Kommunikation zwischen den Gästen und das so wichtige Sehen und Gesehenwerden darstellt.

La trame complexe du paysage urbain contemporain est tissée d'une multitude de lieux où, de plus en plus, l'univers intérieur des espaces publics devient plus important que l'aspect extérieur. Que ce soit pour des raisons de climat, de sécurité, de loisir et de bien-être, les intérieurs, désormais au coeur de l'activité publique, se sont intégrés naturellement à l'itinéraire urbain quotidien.

Tous ces espaces publics sont des lieux d'intenses relations sociales qui se cristallisent dans les bars et les restaurants : propices au flirt et aux rencontres, ils sont aussi sources de divertissement, de détente et permettent de voir et d'être vu. Au fil du temps, ce genre d'établissements s'est forgé sa propre image de marque, s'éloignant ainsi du style impersonnel caractéristique des dernières décennies, pour se métamorphoser en lieux phares imprimés de sceaux différents au gré des relations sociales.

Au fil des pages suivantes, vous trouverez une sélection de bars et restaurants qui, forts de leur design intérieur unique, déterminent l'attitude du visiteur au travers du kaléidoscope riche de sensations issues de leurs ambiances respectives. Entre les formes biologiques étranges du Georges, et les propositions radicales du Shu, un restaurant milanais, une myriade de solutions s'y reflètent à l'infini, pour qui sait observer minutieusement chaque coin et recoin des espaces sélectionnés. Grâce au choix des matériaux employés ou à la disposition des objets de décoration, chaque établissement offre les conditions idéales pour créer, d'une manière ou d'une autre, les échanges entre le public et favoriser l'art de voir et d'être vu.

Entre el gran número de lugares que componen el complejo tejido del paisaje urbano contemporáneo, los espacios públicos interiores cobran cada vez mayor importancia frente al exterior. Ya sea por cuestiones de clima, seguridad, tiempo libre o bienestar, los interiores, como parte de la actividad pública, se han ido incorporando de manera natural al itinerario urbano cotidiano.

La intensidad del intercambio social llevado a cabo en todos estos espacios públicos se concentra en bares y restaurantes: lugar de flirteo y camaradería, de entretenimiento y relajación, de observar y ser observado. Con el tiempo, este tipo de establecimientos ha reclamado un carácter singular propio, alejándose del estilo impersonal que los había definido algunas décadas atrás, y se han convertido en lugares sugerentes que detonan cada anécdota de intercambio social.

Las siguientes páginas muestran una selección de bares y restaurantes que, valiéndose de su particular diseño interior, sugieren al visitante una actitud determinada frente a la amplia gama de sensaciones que desprenden cada uno de los ambientes. Desde las inquietantes formas orgánicas del Georges hasta las radicales propuestas del restaurante milanés Shu, una infinidad de soluciones se reflejan, si se mira con detalle, en cada rincón de estos espacios. Gracias al empleo de los materiales o la disposición de los objetos de decoración, cada local propicia las condiciones para que el intercambio entre el público, la manera de ver y ser visto, se produzca de un modo u otro.

Fra tutti i luoghi che compongono il complesso tessuto urbano contemporaneo, i locali pubblici acquisiscono sempre maggiore importanza rispetto agli spazi all'aperto. Per questioni legate al clima, al tempo libero o al benessere, gli interni come componente dell'attività pubblica sono stati incorporati in modo naturale all'itinerario urbano quotidiano.

L'intensità degli scambi sociali che hanno luogo in questi spazi pubblici è evidente soprattutto nei bar e nei ristoranti, ormai divenuti luoghi di corteggiamento, amicizia, intrattenimento e relazione, dove osservare ed essere osservati. Con il passare del tempo, questi spazi hanno rivendicato un carattere proprio, affrancandosi dallo stile impersonale che li caratterizzava negli anni passati e diventando luoghi suggestivi, ricchi di storia e vita mondana.

Le pagine seguenti mostrano una selezione di bar e ristoranti che, grazie al particolare design degli interni, evocano nel visitatore una vasta gamma di sensazioni. Dalle forme organiche inquietanti del Georges alle proposte radicali del ristorante milanese Shu, ogni angolo di questi spazi riflette un'infinità di soluzioni. Grazie all'attenta scelta dei materiali e alla disposizione degli oggetti decorativi, ogni locale offre condizioni propizie per i rapporti sociali, per vedere ed essere visto, in ogni modo possibile.

America

Brazil

São Paulo   Kosushi
                 Kosushi Restaurant

Colombia

Bogotá   Sayaka
                 Siam
                 Souk

United States

Las Vegas   Lutèce
                 Tsunami

Miami   1220
                 Albion
                 Balanz Café
                 Bed
                 Marlin
                 Mynt
                 Pearl
                 Red Room
                 Sambal Café
                 Touch
                 Wish

New York   Powder
                 The Brasserie

San Francisco   Sno-Drift

Kosushi | Arthur de Mattos Casas

Collaborator: Gilberto Elkis (garden) Photographer: Tuca Reines Chef: George Yuji Koshoji Address: Arthur Ramos Street, São Paulo, Brazil Phone: +55 11 3167 7272 Design concept: The mixture of materials, textures, and references to the Brazilian and Japanese cultures enriches this space, which is inspired by the furnishings from the 50's.

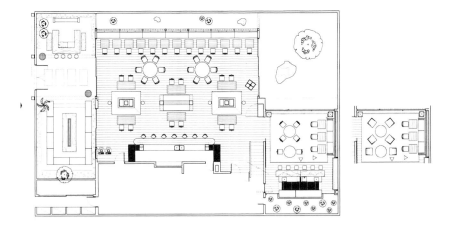

Plan

The Kosushi was conceived as the extension of a restaurant with the same name that has a recognized history in the city. The objective was to create a space that alludes to Japanese design, but does not fall into the typical, traditional Asian style.

Das Kosushi wurde als Erweiterung des gleichnamigen Restaurants konzipiert, das zu den bekanntesten Lokalen der Stadt gehört. Bei der Ausstattung wurde Wert auf japanisches Design gelegt, ohne dass dabei der typisch traditionell-asiatische Stil nachgeahmt wurde.

Le Kosushi est une extension du restaurant du même nom au passé historique connu de la ville. L'idée était de créer un espace inspiré du design japonais sans toutefois tomber dans le style asiatique typique et traditionnel.

El Kosushi se planeó como una extensión del restaurante del mismo nombre, que tiene una historia reconocida en la ciudad. El objetivo era crear un espacio vinculado a referencias japonesas sin caer en los tópicos del estilo tradicional oriental.

Il Koshusi è stato concepito come l'estensione dell'omonimo ristorante che ha fatto la storia della città. L'obiettivo era quello di creare uno spazio che si ispirasse al design giapponese senza cadere nel tipico stile tradizionale asiatico.

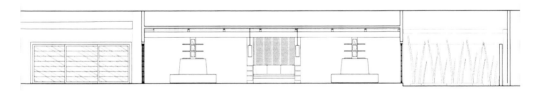

Longitudinal section

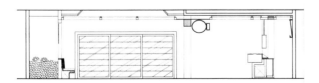

Cross section

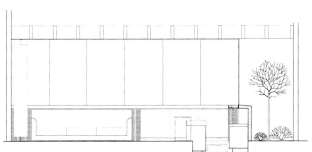

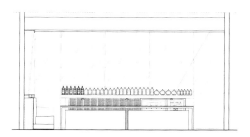

Elevations

Kosushi Restaurant | Arthur de Mattos Casas

Collaborators: Lorenz Acherman, Francisco de Almeida (lighting), and Gilberto Elkis (garden) Photographer: Tuca Reinés Chef: George Yuji Koshoji Address: Arthur Ramos Street, São Paulo, Brazil Phone: +55 11 3167 7272 Design concept: The richness of the interiors is achieved through only a few decorative elements that are both forceful and expressive.

The characteristics of this restaurant demanded a careful intervention that would make the most of the difficult spatial conditions. By combining different materials, the project makes reference to both the traditional Japanese aesthetic and to a contemporary and avant-garde language.

Bei der Gestaltung dieses Restaurants kam es darauf an, mit gut durchdachten Änderungen das Beste aus den schwierigen räumlichen Gegebenheiten zu machen. Die Kombination verschiedener Materialien hat eine gelungene Mischung aus traditioneller japanischer Ästhetik und zeitgenössischer Avantgarde geschaffen.

Les particularités de ce restaurant ont nécessité une étude très approfondie pour optimiser les difficiles conditions spatiales. Grâce à l'alliance de différents matériaux, le projet conjugue l'esthétique japonaise traditionnelle et le langage contemporain d'avant garde.

Las características de este local exigían una intervención cuidadosa que sacara el máximo partido a sus difíciles condiciones espaciales. El proyecto, gracias a la combinación de diferentes materiales, hace referencia tanto a la estética tradicional japonesa como a un lenguaje contemporáneo y vanguardista.

Le caratteristiche di questo ristorante hanno richiesto un intervento attento che sfruttasse al massimo le difficili condizioni spaziali del locale. Combinando i diversi materiali, il progetto allude indirettamente sia all'estetica tradizionale giapponese che al linguaggio avanguardistico contemporaneo.

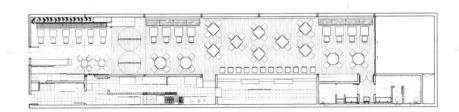

Plan

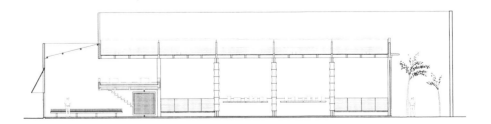

Longitudinal section

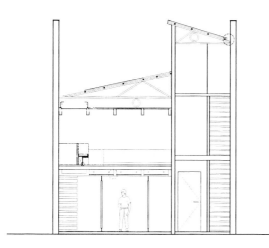

Cross section

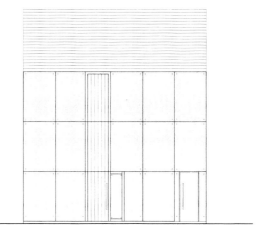

Façade

Sayaka | Giovanny Bautista, Tino Restrepo, Mario Roa, Andrés Casallas

Photographers: **Alejandro Bahamón, Paula Galarza** Address: **Calle 80, 11-16, Bogotá, Colombia** Design concept: **Monochrome palette and advanced lighting systems.**

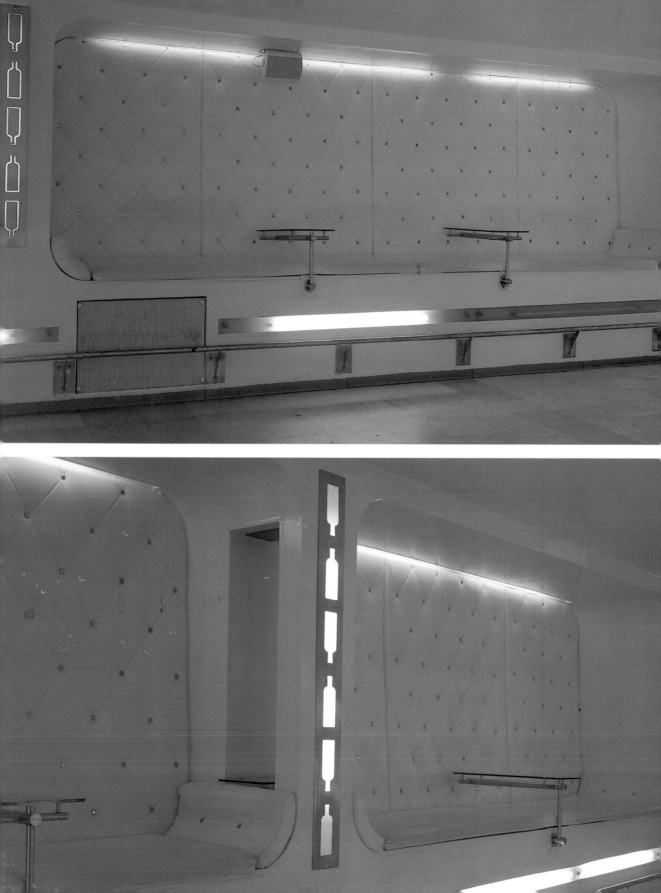

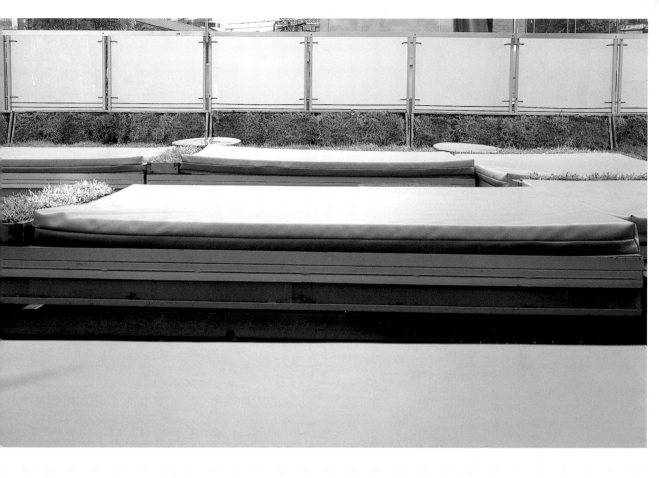

The upper level is a terrace bar and chill out space. It is here that the colors grow warmer –wooden tones of chestnut and beiges–, because of the natural environment. But the terrace combines wood with metal and plastic, thus linking the artful elements of a bar with the natural ones of its location.

Die obere Etage ist eine Terrassenbar mit Chill-out-Bereich. Hier werden die Farben wärmer, kastanienbraune und beigefarbene Holztöne passen sich an die natürliche Umgebung an. Die Terrasse dagegen kombiniert Holz mit Metall und Kunststoff und verbindet die künstlichen Elemente der Bar mit den natürlichen der Umgebung.

L'étage supérieur dispose d'un bar en terrasse et d'un espace chill out. Les couleurs y sont plus chaleureuses –tons de bois déclinant marrons et beiges–, en harmonie avec l'environnement naturel. La terrasse allie bois, métal et plastique créant ainsi un lien entre les éléments artistiques du bar et ceux de la nature environnante.

En la parte superior, la terraza combina bar y chill out. En esta área los tonos se hacen cálidos –colores madera, marrones y beiges–, en consonancia con un espacio natural. La madera convive con el metal y el plástico de manera que conjuga el aire propio de un bar con el ambiente natural en el que se emplaza.

Al livello superiore si trovano un bar con terrazza e un'area chill out. Qui i colori sono più caldi –legno di castagno e del beige–, grazie all'ambientazione naturale. Il legno, accostato a metallo e plastica, contribuisce a integrare in modo ottimale il bar nell'ambiente naturale in cui è collocato.

Siam | Guillermo Arias

Collaborator: Christophe Chavarriat   Photographer: Claudia Uribe/Axxis   Address: Calle 9ª Carrera 2ª Este, Bogotá, Colombia   Design concept: The new and the old combine in an atmosphere of suggestive lights and shadows.

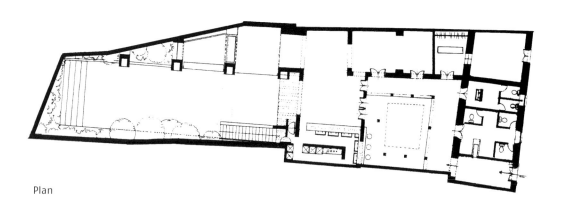

Plan

This bar is located in an ancient colonial house in the old quarter of La Candelaria in Bogotá. The project included all the spaces in the house, as well as the long garden in the back, in a remodeling sought to respect the original structure as much as possible.

Diese Bar liegt in einem alten Haus aus der Kolonialzeit in Bogotas Altstadtviertel La Candelaria. Das Bauprojekt umfasste alle Räume des Hauses und den langen Garten hinter dem Haus. Bei der Neugestaltung wurde darauf geachtet, so viel wie möglich von der ursprünglichen Struktur zu erhalten.

Ce bar se trouve dans une ancienne demeure coloniale, située dans le vieux quartier de La Candeleria à Bogota. Ce projet englobe toutes les pièces de la maison et le long jardin situé à l'arrière de l'édifice, en une remodelage de l'ensemble a été réalisé dans un souci de respecter le plus possible de la structure initiale.

Este bar se encuentra en antigua casa de estilo colonial del barrio de La Candelaria en Bogotá. El proyecto abarca toda la casa, incluido el largo jardín de la parte posterior, en una intervención que ha sido lo más respetuosa posible con la estructura original.

Questo bar si trova in una vecchia casa colonica nell'antico quartiere di La Candelaria a Bogotà. Il progetto ha coinvolto tutti gli spazi della casa e il lungo giardino sul retro, cercando di rispettare la struttura originale nel modo più fedele possibile.

Souk | Guillermo Arias

Photographer: Claudia Uribe/Axxis   Chef: Camilo Giraldo   Address: Carrera 6ª Calle 10ª, Bogotá, Colombia
Design concept: Basic materials and special details mixed with the building's original elements rescue and refresh the historic value of this colonial house.

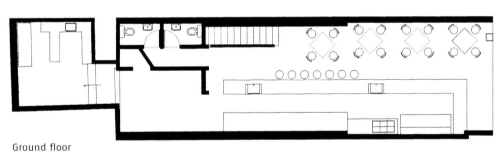

Ground floor

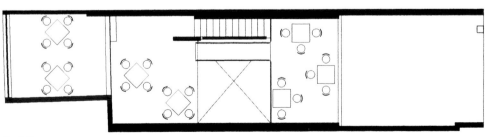

First floor

The restaurant, located in the La Candelaria neighborhood, in the historic center of Bogotá, reconciles all the recent transformations that this area has experienced at time. Basic materials were used to create a dialogue with the building's original character and at the same time give it a contemporary image.

Das Restaurant in Bogotas historischem Altstadtviertel La Candelaria vereint alle Strömungen, die in den letzten Jahren in der Gegend aufgetreten sind. Beim Bau wurden Basismaterialien verwendet, um einen Dialog mit dem ursprünglichen Charakter des Gebäudes herzustellen und gleichzeitig seinen zeitgenössischen Stil zu betonen.

Le restaurant, proche de La Candeleria, situé dans le centre historique de Bogota, réunit toutes les transformations que cet quartier traversée au long des anées. Les matériaux de base ont été choisis pour entrer en dialogue avec le caractère original de l'édifice tout en lui conférant une image contemporaine.

El restaurante, ubicado en La Candelaria, el barrio histórico de Bogotá, concilia las múltiples transformaciones de las que ha sido objeto esta zona con el tiempo. Se incorporaron materiales básicos que dialogan con el carácter original de la casa al tiempo que dan una imagen contemporánea.

Il ristorante, collocato in La Candelaria, il quartiere storico di Bogotà, concilia le diverse trasformazioni che l'area ha subito nel tempo. Sono stati utilizzati materiali di base che dialogano con il carattere originale della casa conferendole un'immagine contemporanea.

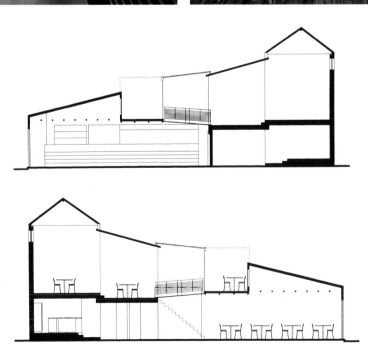

Sections

Lutèce | Morphosis

Photographer: Farshid Assassi Chef: David Fean Address: 3355 S Las Vegas Boulevard, Las Vegas, Nevada, US
Phone: +1 702 414 2220 Design concept: Organic forms, geometric shapes and angled structures.

3D model

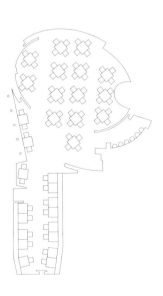

Ground floor

A bronze wall in the form of an elliptical cone wraps around the dining room, functioning as a gesture that organizes the general space. A glass surface around this piece both connects and divides the restaurant from the bar and the entrance.

Eine bronzene Wand in Form eines elliptischen Kegels verläuft um den Speisesaal und teilt den Raum auf. Eine rundherum laufende Glasfläche dient als Verbindungs- und zugleich Trennungselement zwischen Restaurant und Bar bzw. Eingangsbereich.

Un mur de bronze en forme de cône elliptique s'enroule autour de la salle à manger et fait fonction d'élément central dans l'organisation de l'espace. Cet ouvrage est entouré d'une surface de verre qui relie le restaurant au bar tout en le séparant.

Una pared de bronce en forma de cono elíptico envuelve el comedor y constituye el elemento que organiza el espacio general. Una paramento de cristal que rodea esta pieza conecta la entrada y el bar con el restaurante.

Una parete di bronzo a forma di cono ellittico avvolge la sala da pranzo e organizza lo spazio generale. Un paravento di cristallo intorno a questo pezzo collega l'entrata e il bar con il ristorante.

General plan

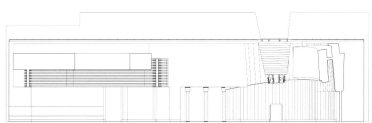

Longitudinal section

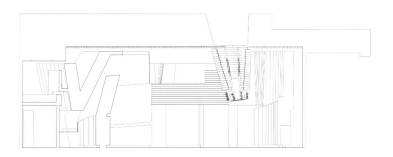

Cross section

Tsunami | Morphosis

Collaborators: Thom Mayne, Rebecca Méndez Photographer: Farshid Assassi Chef: José Trinidad Address: 3377 Boulevard South, Las Vegas, Nevada, US Phone: +1 702 414 1980 Design concept: The main inspirations of this restaurant are the original elements of a classic salon-dining room together with references to the formal chaos of Las Vegas casinos.

Ground floor

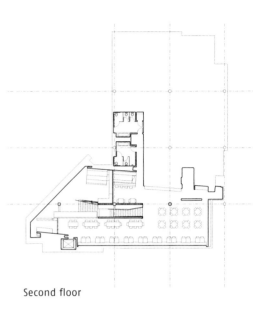

Second floor

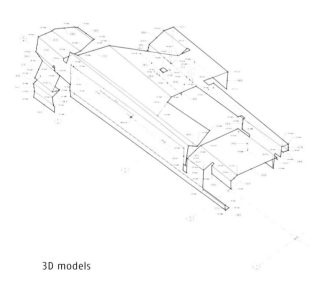

3D models

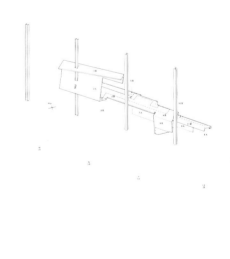

The objective of the interior design of Tsunami, which specializes in Asian cuisine, was to create a space that spotlights the decor and the exquisite menu of specialties. Morphosis´s idea was to find an intriguing balance between the immateriality of the two-dimensional image and the three-dimensional space.

Ziel des Innendesigns des auf asiatische Küche spezialisierten Tsunami war es, einen Ort zu schaffen, an dem sowohl Dekor als auch exquisite Spezialitäten im Vordergrund stehen. Morphosis strebte mit diesem Projekt ein Gleichgewicht zwischen der Immaterialität zwei-dimensionaler Bilder und drei-dimensionaler Räume an.

Le design intérieur du Tsunami, spécialisé dans la cuisine asiatique, visait à créer un espace mettant l'accent sur le décor et les spécialités exquises. Morphosis voulait trouver un équilibre intéressant entre le symbole bi dimensionnel et l'espace tri dimensionnel.

El objetivo principal a la hora de diseñar los interiores de este restaurante especializado en cocina asiática era convertir la decoración y la exquisita carta de especialidades en protagonistas. Morphosis pretendía encontrar el equilibrio entre la imagen bi-dimensional y el espacio tridimensional.

L'obiettivo principale dell'organizzazione degli interni allo Tsunami, specializzato in cucina asiatica, era quello di mettere al centro del ristorante le decorazioni e l'eccezionale menu. Morphosis ha inteso creare un particolare equilibrio tra l'immagine a due dimensioni del locale e lo spazio tridimensionale.

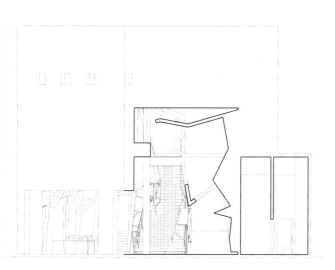

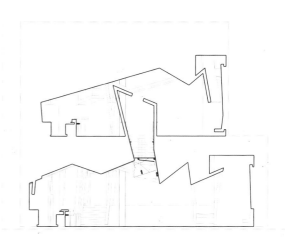

Sections

Collaborator: John Pringle Photographer: Pep Escoda Chef: Roger Ruch Address: The Tides Hotel, 1220 Ocean Drive, Miami Beach, Florida, US Phone: +1 305 604 5130 Design concept: The integration of contemporary furnishings withinin a predominantly Art Déco style.

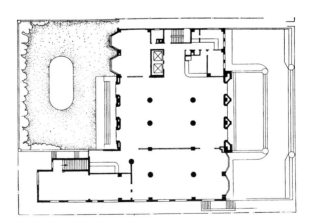

Plan

This restaurant forms part of the hotel The Tides, originally designed by architect L. Murria Dixon in 1936 and remodeled in 1977. The interior was updated with contemporary furniture, while the armchairs and the circular lamps that illuminate the bar retain certain Art Déco features.

Dieses Restaurant gehört zu der Hotelanlage des The Tides, die 1936 von dem Architekten L. Murria Dixon entworfen und im Jahre 1977 renoviert wurde. Zeitgenössische Möbel ersetzten das alte Mobiliar, wenn auch die Sessel sowie die kreisförmigen Lampen an der Bar immer noch für ein gewisses Art-Déco-Flair sorgen.

Ce restaurant fait partie du hôtel The Tides, déjà conçu en 1936 par l'architecte L. Murria Dixon et remodelé ensuite en 1977. L'intérieur a été modernisé à l'aide d'un mobilier contemporain mais conserve également les accents Art Déco des fauteuils et des lampes circulaires qui éclairent le bar.

Este restaurante forma parte del hotel The Tides y fue originariamente diseñado por el arquitecto L. Murria Dixon en 1936 y remodelado en 1977. El interior se ha modernizado con muebles contemporáneos, aunque los sillones y las lámparas circulares que iluminan la barra conservan algunos rasgos Art Déco.

Questo ristorante appartiene all'hotel The Tides, progettato originariamente dall'architetto L. Murria Dixon e rimodellato nel 1977. Gli interni sono stati modernizzati con mobili contemporanei, mentre le poltrone e le lampade circolari che illuminano il bar conservano alcune reminiscenze dello stile Art Déco.

Albion | Propeller Z

Collaborators: Rubell family Photographer: Pep Escoda Address: 1650 James Avenue, Miami Beach, Florida, US Phone: +1 305 913 3000 Design concept: This bar features a contrast between different materials and textures, incorporating both classic and contemporary elements.

The formal language of the interior could be defined as a program of folds, imbalances, and ruptures of the materials. Each architectural element, including the columns, the ceiling, and the walls, breaks apart and forms fissures and transparencies that enrich the space.

Die formelle Sprache des Interieurs lässt sich definieren als Kombination aus Biegungen, Ungleichgewichten und Verwendung unterschiedlichster Materialien. Jedes Bauelement, einschließlich Säulen, Decke und Wände, bricht ab und erzeugt Risse und Transparenzen, die den Raum bereichern.

Le langage formel de l'intérieur se définit comme un système de plis, de déséquilibres et de ruptures de matériaux. Chaque élément architectural, à l'instar des colonnes, du plafond et des murs, se brise créant des fissures et des transparences qui enrichissent l'espace.

El lenguaje formal del interior se puede definir como un temario de pliegues y desniveles de los materiales. Cada elemento arquitectónico, como las columnas, el techo o las paredes, se descompone dando lugar a fisuras y transparencias que enriquecen un espacio de forma regular y reducidas proporciones.

Il linguaggio formale degli interni si esprime tramite le pieghe e i dislivelli dei materiali. Ogni elemento architettonico, dalle colonne, al soffitto fino ai muri, si scompone dando forma a fessure e trasparenze che arricchiscono lo spazio.

Balanz Café | Sedley Place Designers

Photographer: Pep Escoda Address: 1022 Lincoln Road, Miami, Florida, US Phone: +1 305 534 9191 Design concept: Zebra patterns and bright colors breath life into this modern restaurant and café.

The Balanz is situated in Miami Beach, in a bustling commercial, gaming, and cultural activities area. The semicircular bar, presided over by a large mirror that reflects much of the café, organizes the space into two sections, one being the café and the other the seating area, with chairs and tables for restaurant service.

Das Balanz liegt inmitten des pulsierenden Geschäfts-, Spiel- und Kulturlebens von Miami Beach. Über der halbrunden Theke hängt ein großer Spiegel, in dem ein großer Teil des Cafés reflektiert wird. Der Raum ist in zwei Bereiche geteilt: in ein Café und einen Restaurantbereich mit Tischen und Stühlen.

Le Balanz est situé dans Miami Beach, à une zone bouillonnante d'activités commerciales, ludiques et culturelles. Le bar en hémicycle, surmonté d'un immense miroir reflétant une grande partie de la vie du café, organise l'espace en deux parties : le café d'un côté et de l'autre, une zone assise pour la restauration, agrémentée de tables et chaises.

El Balanz se encuentra situado en Miami Beach, en una zona de atractivo interés turístico y rodeado de una bulliciosa actividad comercial, lúdica y cultural. La barra semicircular, presidida por un espejo que refleja gran parte del local, organiza el espacio en dos secciones, una destinada a café y otra en la que se han distribuido mesas para poder ofrecer un servicio de restaurante.

Il Balanz si trova a Miami Beach, in una zona con interessanti attrazioni turistiche, commerciali e culturali. Il bar semicircolare, con un grande specchio che riflette gran parte del locale, divide lo spazio in due, separando il caffè dalla zona ristorante con tavoli e sedie.

Bed | Oliver & Pascale Hoyos

Photographer: Pep Escoda Chef: Vitor Casassola Address: 929 Washington Av, Miami Beach, Florida, US
Phone: +1 305 532 9070 Design concept: A delicate setting with subtle romantic references for a repertoire
of music, food and entertainment.

The principle behind the design of Bed was to create a comfortable and intimate atmosphere that reflects a hedonistic culture. Bed offers the visitor luxurious and pleasurable surroundings, as well as a studied collection of music, entertainment, and first-class gourmet cuisine.

Bei der Gestaltung des Bed war die Idee, eine komfortabel ausgestattete und intime Atmosphäre zu schaffen, die eine hedonistische Kultur reflektieren sollte. Bed bietet dem Gast eine luxuriöse und angenehme Umgebung und eine gelungen komponierte Kombination aus Musik, Unterhaltung und erstklassiger Gourmet-Küche.

L'idée derrière le design du Bed est de créer une ambiance intime et conviviale qui reflète l'hédonisme. Le Bed offre un environnement agréable et plaisant doté d'une sélection étudiée de morceaux de musique, d'un programme de variété et d'une cuisine pour fins gourmets, de première classe.

El principio del diseño del Bed era forjar un ambiente íntimo que recreara la cultura hedonista. El Bed ofrece al visitante un entorno de lujo y placer junto con una estudiada colección de música, entretenimiento y comida gourmet de primer orden.

Il principio a cui si ispira il design del Bed è la creazione di uno spazio intimo e attento alla cultura edonista. Il Bed offre al visitatore un ambiente piacevole e sensuale e che lo vizi con un'attenta combinazione di musica, intrattenimenti e cucina di alto livello.

Marlin | Barbara Hulanicky

Photographer: Pep Escoda Address: 1200 Collins Avenue, Miami, Florida, US Phone: +1 305 604 5063 Design concept: An extensive use of stainless steel coupled with cool grey tones and Art Déco motifs.

A historic building that dates from 1939 and whose lines are ruled by the regulations that define the Art Déco style, its rehabilitation and transformation has been achieved by arranging warm, functional spaces where the trends of the cutting edge of design are present in every corner.

Ein historisches Gebäude aus dem Jahre 1939, dessen Linien durch die Regeln des Art-deco-Stils bestimmt sind, wurde gelungen saniert und zu einem warmen, funktionalen Ort umgebaut, in dem die neuesten Designtrends allgegenwärtig sind.

Ce monument historique, datant de 1939, aux lignes définies par les canons de l'Art Déco, a été réhabilité et transformé en y aménageant des espaces chaleureux et fonctionnels où les dernières tendances du design se nichent partout.

La rehabilitación de un edificio histórico de 1939 cuyos trazos se rigen por las directrices que definen el estilo Art Déco ha conseguido delimitar unos espacios acogedores y funcionales en los que las tendencias más actuales invaden todos los rincones.

Questo edificio storico dalle linee Art Déco risalente al 1939 è stato ristrutturato e trasformato creando spazi accoglienti e funzionali, dove le tendenze più attuali del design sono visibili ad ogni angolo.

Mynt | Juan Carlos Arcila-Duque

Photographer: Pep Escoda Chef: Luciano Santo Address: 1921 Collins Avenue, Miami Beach, Florida, US Phone: +1 786 276 6132 Design concept: Minimalist design and the incorporation of indirect lighting techniques.

Mynt's decorative concept lies in a new generation of club-goers in Miami. The architect was inspired by architectural elements and materials from time in New York, and Mynt's location, which is what sparked the retro style.

Die Gestaltung des Mynt ist ganz nach dem Geschmack des jüngeren Publikums der Nachtszene Miami's gestaltet. Der Architekt hat sich bei der Verwendung der architektonischen Elemente und Materialien von seinem Aufenthalt in New York inspirieren lassen, den ursprünglichen Charakter des Ortes hat er allerdings auch nicht außer Acht gelassen: Ein Hauch von Retro ist hier noch zu spüren.

Le concept de décoration du Mynt se base sur une nouvelle génération de clientèle nocturne à Miami. Le architecte s'est inspiré à la fois d'éléments architecturaux et de matériaux inspirés de sa période New-yorkaise et du lieu de l'établissement donnant naissance au style rétro.

El concepto base de la decoración del Mynt se apoya en una nueva generación de público nocturno de Miami. El arquitecto se ha inspirado en los elementos arquitectónicos y materiales provenientes de su etapa en Nueva York, y también en el pasado del establecimiento, que ha aportado el estilo retro del local.

Il concetto decorativo del Mynt si rivolge alla nuova generazione del popolo della notte di Miami. Il architetto si è ispirato agli elementi architettonici e ai materiali di New York ma anche alla storia del Mynt. Il locale, infatti, ha riacquistato lo stile retró del passato.

Pearl Stephan Bupoux

Photographer: Pep Escoda Chef: Frank Jeanetti Address: 1 Ocean Drive, Miami, Florida, US Phone: +1 305 538 1111 Design concept: The sophistication of this ambience is achieved through homogeneous, daring lighting that dominates the space.

The furnishings in the dining room were inspired by American cafés of the 40's and 50's, in a salute to the golden age of Miami's Art Deco district. The bar stools recall the Futurism of the 60's and 70's, while the low sofas also create a variety of situations within the same warm atmosphere.

Die Einrichtung des Speisesaals war inspiriert an den amerikanischen Cafés der 40er und 50er Jahre in einer Verbeugung vor dem goldenen Zeitalter von Miamis Art-Déco-Viertel. Die Barhocker erinnern an den Futurismus der 60er und 70er Jahre, während die niedrigen Sofas inmitten einer warmen Atmosphäre sorgen.

L'ameublement de la salle à manger s'inspire des cafés américains des années quarante et cinquante en hommage à l'âge d'or du district Art Déco de Miami. Les tabourets de bar rappellent le futurisme des années soixante et soixante dix alors que les divans bas créent une multitude de situations baignées de la même atmosphère chaleureuse.

El mobiliario del comedor se inspira en las cafeterías americanas de los años cuarenta y cincuenta, y hace referencia a la época dorada del distrito Art Déco de Miami. Las sillas de la barra hacen alusión al futurismo de los años sesenta y setenta, mientras que los sofás bajos ofrecen una gran variedad de posibilidades dentro de una misma atmósfera cálida.

I mobili nella sala da pranzo si ispirano ai caffè americani degli anni quaranta e cinquanta, in un omaggio all'età aurea del quartiere art déco di Miami. Gli sgabelli del bar ricordano il futurismo degli anni sessanta e settanta, mentre i divani bassi contribuiscono a differenziare l'ambiente senza compromettere la sua atmosfera accogliente.

Red Room | Anda Andrei

Photographer: Pep Escoda Address: The Shore Club, 1901 Collins Avenue, Miami Beach, Florida, US Phone: +1 305 695 3100 Design concept: An exotic atmosphere of rich textures, deep red tones, contrasting textures and unique lighting effects.

The combination of classic and modern balances the design in an atemporal environment: a pool table covered in stainless steel and upholstered in red, chairs in silvery Indian prints, silver trays, and glass chandeliers make for a theatrical environment.

Durch die ausgewogene Kombination von klassischem und modernem Mobiliar entsteht der Eindruck einer zeitlosen Umgebung: Ein Edelstahl verkleideter Billardtisch mit rotem Bezug, bunt bedruckte Sessel aus Indien, Silbertabletts sowie auch die gläsernen Kronleuchter schaffen eine nahezu theatrale Atmosphäre.

Le mélange de mobilier classique et moderne donne un design harmonieux dans une atmosphère intemporelle : une table de billard plaquée d'acier inoxydable au tapis rouge, des chaises recouvertes de tissage argenté d'Inde, plateaux d'argent ou chandeliers de cristal créent une ambiance théâtrale.

La combinación de muebles clásicos y modernos equilibra el diseño en una atmósfera atemporal: una mesa de billar chapada de acero inoxidable con tapiz de color rojo, sillas estampadas con tejidos plateados de la India, bandejas de plata o candelabros de cristal componen un ambiente muy teatral.

La combinazione di classico e moderno conferisce un equilibrio particolare al design del locale collocandolo in un'atmosfera senza tempo: un tavolo da biliardo rivestito in acciaio inossidabile con tappeto rosso, le sedie con stampe indiane argentate, i vassoi d'argento e i candelabri di vetro creano un ambiente decisamente teatrale.

Sambal Café | Tony Chi

Photographer: **Pep Escoda** Chef: **Paul Miller** Address: **500 Brikell Key Drive, Miami, Florida, US** Phone: **+1 305 913 8251** Design concept: **Tropical meets urban in this chic and relaxing bar in Miami.**

A subtle Oriental elegance blended with Occidental airs runs through the different rooms of the Sambal Café. An agreeable mestizo aesthetic defines this establishment located inside the Hotel Mandarin Oriental, in one of the most prestigious residential and business zones of Miami.

Die Atmosphäre des Sambal Café ist gekennzeichnet durch eine unaufdringliche Eleganz orientalischen Stils vermischt mit westlichen Anklängen. Das Lokal besticht durch eine angenehme Mischung unterschiedlicher ästhetischer Stile. Es liegt im Hotel Mandarin Oriental in einem der renommiertesten Wohn- und Einkaufsviertel von Miami.

Une subtile élégance orientale tamisée, aux allures occidentales, parcourt les différents espaces du Sambal Café. Une esthétique métissée agréable caractérise cet établissement, situé à l'intérieur de l'Hôtel Mandarin Oriental, dans une des plus prestigieuses zones résidentielles et commerciales de Miami.

Una sutil elegancia oriental tamizada con aires occidentales recorre las diferentes áreas que conforman el Sambal Café. Una agradable estética mestiza define este establecimiento, ubicado en el interior del Hotel Mandarin Oriental, en una de las zonas residenciales y comerciales más prestigiosas de Miami.

Una delicata eleganza orientale filtrata da arie occidentali percorre i diversi ambienti del Sambal Café. Una gradevole estetica meticcia definisce questo locale, situato dentro l'Hotel Mandarin Oriental, in una delle zone residenziali e commerciali di maggior prestigio di Miami.

Touch | Stephane Dupoux

Photographer: Pep Escoda Chef: Sean Brasel Address: 910 Licoln Road, Miami Beach, Florida, US Phone: +1 305 532 8003 Design concept: Predominant use of wood and steel.

The Caribbean context that Miami Beach provides inspires the decorating: lively shapes, thrills of nature and exuberant elegance. Stephane Dupoux designed the club with upbeat sophistication and theatrical lighting and both aspects combines fun and elegance.

Das Karibik-Element von Miami Beach diente als Inspiration bei der Einrichtung: lebendige Formen, Naturschönheiten und überwältigende Eleganz. Stephane Dupoux hat den Club mit Pep und Raffinesse entworfen und eine Theaterbeleuchtung vorgesehen. Das Ergebnis ist eine gut durchdachte Szenerie, die Spaß und Eleganz vereint.

L'ambiance des Caraïbes de Miami Beach se retrouve dans la décoration : formes ondoyantes, exaltation de la nature et élégance dans l'exubérance. Stéphane Dupoux a réalisé pour le club un design qui allie raffinement extrême et éclairage théâtral e ces deux aspects créent amusement et élégance.

El contexto caribeño de Miami Beach inspira la decoración: formas afiladas, exaltación de la naturaleza y elegancia en la exuberancia. Stephane Dupoux ha dotado al local de una lúdica sofisticación e iluminación teatral y ambos aspectos aúnan diversión y elegancia.

Il contesto caraibico di Miami Beach ha ispirato la decorazione: forme affilate, esaltazione della naturalezza e eleganza nell'esuberanza di questo bar. Stephane Dupoux ha dotato il locale di un gusto ludico ma sofisticato e di un'illuminazione teatrale e entrambi gli aspetti contribuiscono coniugan divertimento e stile.

Wish | Beilinson Architects

Collaborator: Orlando Comas (landscape architect) Photographer: Pep Escoda Chef: Michael Borse Address: The Hotel 801, Collins Avenue, Miami Beach, Florida, US Phone: +1 305 531 2222 Design concept: An Art Déco theme remains a constant in all the structural and decorative details present in this space.

This elegant restaurant designed by Beilinson architectural studio forms part of The Tiffany. In 1939, architect L. Murria Dixon built the original edifice, which today counts among the group of historic hotels in the United States.

Dieses elegante Restaurant gehört zum Hotel The Tiffany, das nach den Entwürfen des Architekturbüros Beilinson errichtet wurde. Die Anlage war ursprünglich im Jahre 1939 von dem Architekten L. Murria Dixon konzipiert worden und gehört heute zu einer Hotelgruppe historischer Hotels in den Vereinigten Staaten.

Ce restaurant élégant, conçu par les studios d'architecture Beilinson, fait partie de l'hôtel The Tiffany. Cet édifice, construit en 1939 par l'architecte L. Murria Dixon, fait partie aujourd'hui de l'ensemble des hôtels historiques des Etats-Unis.

Este elegante restaurante forma parte del hotel The Tiffany, concebido por el estudio de Beilinson. La edificación fue construida originariamente en 1939 por el arquitecto L. Murria Dixon y forma parte, hoy en día, del conjunto de hoteles históricos de Estados Unidos.

Questo elegante ristorante progettato dallo studio di architettura Beilinson fa parte del hotel The Tiffany. Nel 1939 l'architetto L. Murria Dixon costruì l'edificio originale, che oggi appartiene al gruppo degli hotel storici degli Stati Uniti.

Powder | Karim Rashid

Collaborators: J. Sahba, C. Tariki Photographer: Ramin Talaie Address: 431 W 16th Street, New York, US
Phone: +1 212 229 9119 Design concept: Custom-designed furniture, modern materials and a futuristic
aesthic characterize this contemporary space.

The Powder is a futurist remnant in the city of all cities: New York. The main elements of the design are the color and the organic shapes that infuse the space. Karim Rashid designed the furnishings for the bar and the DJ booth: water and fireproof purple vinyl seats with orange backrests.

Das Powder ist das futuristische Wagnis in der Stadt aller Städte: New York. Farben und organische Formen bestimmen die Innenausstattung dieses New Yorker Lokals. Karim Rashid entwarf das Mobiliar der Theke und der DJ-Kabine sowie zum Beispiel die wasser- und feuerfesten knallroten Vinylsessel mit orangefarbenen Rückenlehnen.

Le Powder est un vestige futuriste dans la cité de toutes les cités : New York. Les éléments plus importants du design sont la couleur et les formes organiques qui scandent l'espace. Karim Rashid est l'auteur du design du mobilier et de la cabine du DJ : sièges de vinyle pourpre, ignifugés et imperméabilisés avec dos en vinyle orange.

El Powder es un retazo futurista en la ciudad de las ciudades: Nueva York. Los elementos principales del diseño son el color y las formas orgánicas que organizan el espacio. El mobiliario de los bares y la cabina del DJ es un diseño de Karim Rashid, con asientos de vinilo púrpura y respaldos de vinilo naranja.

Il Powder è un retaggio futurista nella città delle città: New York. Gli elementi più significativi del design sono il colore e le forme organiche nello spazio. Karim Rashid ha progettato i mobili del bar e della cabina dj, dove ha collocato sedie ignifughe in vinile viola con schienale arancio.

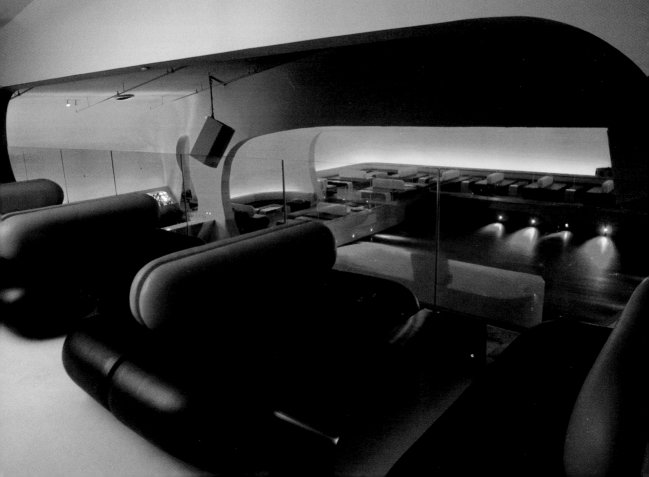

The Brasserie | Diller & Scofidio

Collaborators: Ben Rubin (video), Alan Burden (structures), Richard Saber (lighting), Mary Bright (curtains), Douglas Cooper (installations) Photographer: Michael Moran Chef: Luc Dimnet Address: 100 East 53rd Street, New York, US Phone: +1 212 751 4840 Design concept: In tribute to the former The Brasserie, the architects preserved the descent from street level to the floor of the dining room and exaggerated it by adding a grand staircase with glass steps.

The Seagram building is one of the architectural paradigms of the Modern Movement. To achieve the contemporary and timeless spirit that skyscrapers exemplify, the project was carried out according to the principles—and challenges—of rationalism.

Das Seagram-Gebäude ist eines der Paradigmen der Moderne. Um den zeitgenössischen und gleichzeitig zeitlosen Geist von Wolkenkratzern zu veranschaulichen, wurde dieses Projekt nach den Prinzipien und Herausforderungen des Rationalismus konzipiert.

L'édifice Seagram est un des paradigmes architecturaux du Mouvement Moderne. Pour atteindre l'esprit contemporain et intemporel représenté par les gratte ciels, le projet a été réalisé selon les principes – et les défis - du rationalisme.

El edificio Seagram es uno de los paradigmas arquitectónicos del movimiento moderno. Para conseguir un espíritu contemporáneo y a la vez atemporal que representan los rascacielos, el proyecto siguió los principios –y los desafíos– de racionalismo.

L'edificio Seagram è uno dei paradigmi architettonici del Movimento Moderno. Per celebrare lo spirito contemporaneo ma senza tempo esemplificato dai grattacieli, il progetto è stato eseguito secondo i principi –e le sfide– del razionalismo.

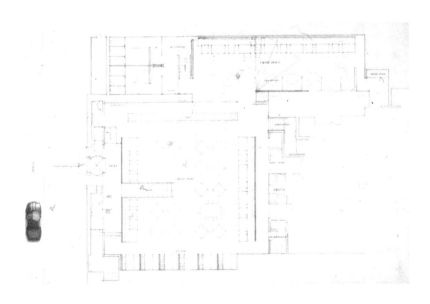

Ground floor

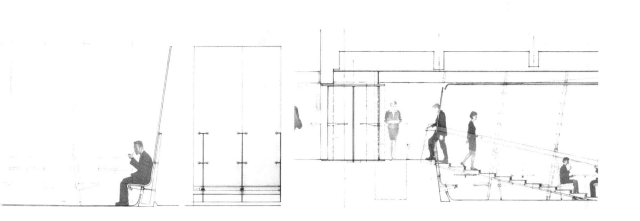

Detailed sections

147

Sno-Drift | Charles Doell & Craige Walters

Photographer: Tatiana Brockmann Chef: Paul Curley Address: 1830 3rd Street, San Francisco, California, US Phone: +1 415 431 4766 Design concept: A mix of retro, contemporary and kitsch styles make up the interior design of this club.

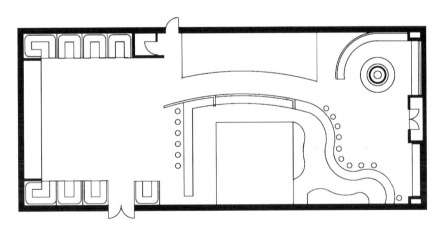

Plan

The club is a mixture of styles that combines glamour and kitsch and creates a new aesthetic we might call Sno-Chic with Alpine elements like the fawn and fireplace in the bar. The design aims to create an ambience that exudes positive feelings.

Der Club ist eine Stilmischung, die Glamour und Kitsch kombiniert und eine neue Ästhetik schafft, der man den Namen Sno-Chic geben könnte. Besonders originell sind die Alpenelemente wie das Rehkitz und der Kamin in der Bar. Das Design war darauf ausgerichtet, eine komfortabel ausgestattete Umgebung zu schaffen, die beim Gast eine positive Stimmung erzeugt.

Le club est un mélange de styles alliant élégance et kitsch tout en créant une esthétique nouvelle que l'on pourrait qualifier de « sno-chic » intégrant dans le bar des éléments alpins comme le faon et la cheminée. Le design vise à créer un environnement où le client se love dans une ambiance dégageant des ondes positives.

El local es una mezcla de estilos que combina el glamour y lo kitsch, y crea una nueva estética que puede ser descrita como "sno-chic", con elementos alpinos como el cervatillo y la chimenea instalados en el bar. El objetivo era crear una atmósfera que destila sensaciones positivas.

Il locale è un miscuglio di stili che combina il glamour e il kitsch in una nuova estetica che può essere descritta come "sno-chic", con elementi alpini come il cerbiatto e il caminetto del bar. Il progetto intende creare un ambiente che avvolga il cliente trasmettendogli sensazioni positive.

Australia / Asia

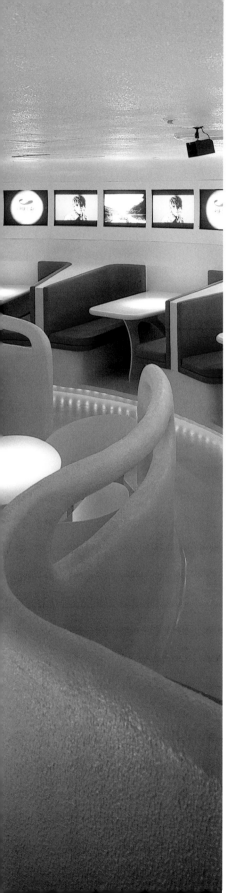

Australia

Melbourne	Bond Bar
	EQ
	FFour
	Lotus
	Pelican
	Salon Rouge
Sydney	Cruise Bar & Restaurant
	Guillaume at Bennelong Restaurant

China

Hong Kong	Dragon-i

Israel

Tel-Aviv	TLV

Japan

Tokyo	J-Pop Odaiba
	Moph

Bond Bar | Playground

Photographer: Shania Shegedyn Chefs: Berlinda George, Joshua James, Aaron Anderson and Lou Trajkov
Address: 24 Bond Street, Melbourne, Australia Phone: +613 9629 9844 Design concept: The seamless
design of the banquette seating is the most notable aspect of this bar in Melbourne.

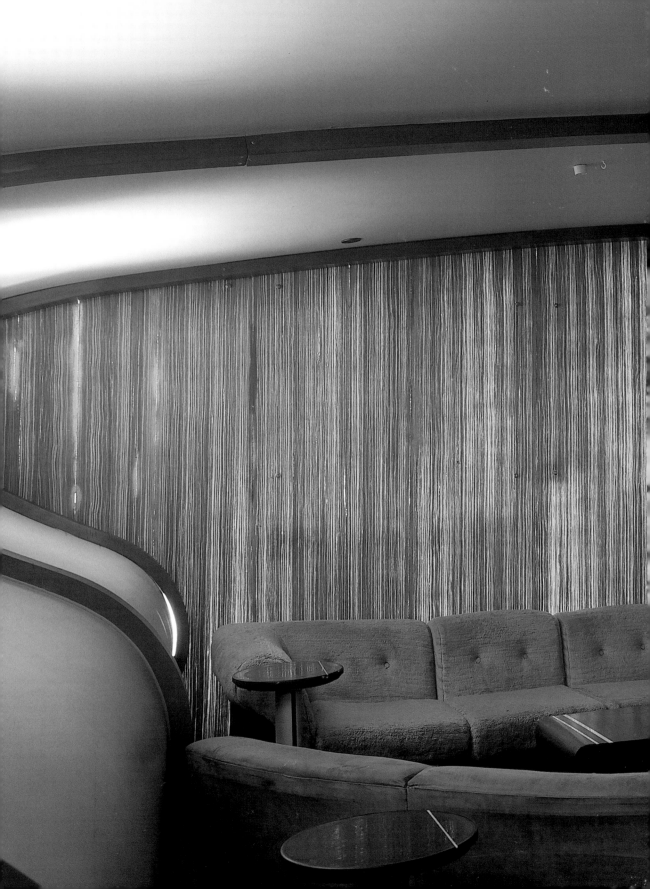

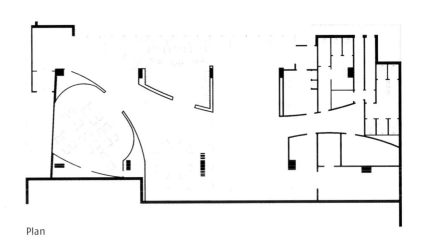

Plan

Sensuality and good mood defines this club situated in downtown Melbourne. The space stands out visually due to the influence of Art Déco, on the one hand, and minimalism on the other. In fact, the aesthetic of the bar stems from the combination of art and design.

Sinnlichkeit und gute Laune stehen im Vordergrund in diesem Lokal in der Innenstadt von Melbourne. Bei der Ausstattung der Räume dominieren Elemente des Art-Déco auf der einen Seite und minimalistische Stilelemente auf der anderen. Die Ästhetik des Lokals resultiert aus der gelungenen Mischung von Kunst und Design.

Sensualité et bonne humeur caractérisent ce club situé au cœur de Melbourne. L'espace est sous la double influence de l'Art Déco et du minimalisme. L'esthétique du bar naît de l'alliance entre art et design.

Sensualidad y buen humor caracterizan este local situado en el centro de Melbourne. El diseño del espacio destaca visualmente por la influencia estilística del Art Déco, por un lado, y del minimalismo, por otro. De hecho, la estética del bar nace de la combinación de arte y diseño.

Sensuali e buon umore caraterizzano questo locale nel centro di Melbourne. Il disegno dello spazio presenta da un lato i tratti marcati dell'Art Déco, e dall'altro una buona dose di minimalismo. Non a caso, l'estetica del bar nasce da una combinazione unica tra arte e design.

Collaborators: Connel Wagner (structural engineering), Bassett Consulting (installations) Photographers: Lucinda McLean, Peter Bennetts, Lyn Pool Chef: Bernard McCarthy Address: 100 St Kilda Road, Melbourne, Australia Phone: +613 9645 0644 Design concept: The combined use of raw wood and polished metal generate a simple yet impressive terrace bar.

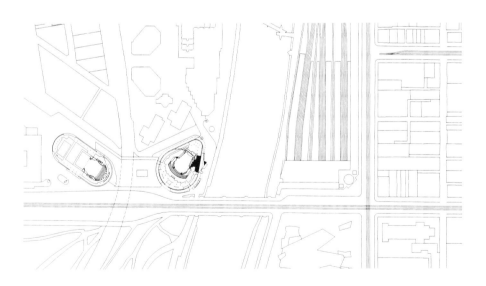

Location plan

The project focused on adapting the establishment to its location along the Yarra River, in the heart of Melbourne. The objective was to create a place for people of all sorts, assuming, at the same time, a commitment both to civic responsibility and the market potential of the establishment.

Bei diesem Projekt im Zentrum von Melbourne stand die Anpassung an die Lage am Fluss Yarra im Vordergrund. Es sollte ein Aufenthaltsort für Menschen jeden Typs entstehen, bei dem gleichzeitig die Verpflichtung zur Bürgerverantwortung sowie das kommerzielle Potential wichtig waren.

Le but du projet était d'adapter cet établissement à sa situation le long de la Yarra River, au cœur de Melbourne. L'objectif était de créer un endroit ouvert à une clientèle très diverse tout en s'engageant à assurer la combinaison entre responsabilités civiles et potentiel commercial de l'établissement.

El proyecto de este restaurante requería la adaptación del establecimiento a su ubicación junto al río Yarra, en el centro de Melbourne. La intención era concebir un lugar para todo tipo de gente y comprometido con la responsabilidad cívica y el potencial comercial de la implantación.

Il progetto di questo ristorante prevedeva l'adattamento della costruzione all'ambiente circostante lungo il fiume Yarra, nel centro di Melbourne. L'obiettivo era la creazione di un luogo per persone di ogni genere, senza trascurare la responsabilità civile e il potenziale commerciale dell'edificio.

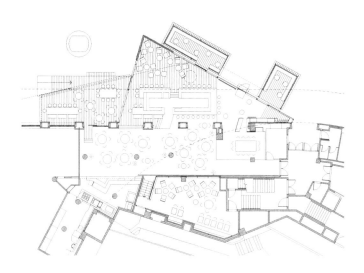

Ground plan

FFour | Playground

Photographer: Derek Swallwell Chef: Marcus Motteram Address: 318-322 Little Collins Street, Melbourne, Australia Design concept: Ultra-modern forms are fused with retro furnishings and patterns in this decidedly original space.

The architectural approach is instinctive and experimental; some of the techniques used are repetition, perspective and unity. The space is shaped like a symmetrical diamond with a convex roof; the walls are angled, and the floor and ceiling meet to form a false perspective.

Der architektonische Ansatz ist von Instinkt und Experimentierfreude geleitet. Zu den eingesetzten Techniken gehören Wiederholung, Perspektive und Einheit. Der Raum ist in Form eines symmetrischen Diamanten mit konvexem Dach gestaltet. Die Wände sind verwinkelt, und Gelände und Decke treffen aufeinander und erzeugen eine falsche Perspektive.

L'approche architecturale est à la fois instinctive et expérimentale ; répétition, perspective et unité sont au nombre des techniques utilisées. L'espace a la forme d'un diamant symétrique avec un toit convexe. Les murs sont anguleux, le sol et le plafond se rejoignent pour former une fausse perspective.

La aproximación a la arquitectura es instintiva y experimental; algunos de los recursos utilizados son la repetición, la perspectiva y la unidad. El espacio adquiere la forma de un diamante simétrico de techo convexo; las paredes en ángulo, el techo y el suelo convergen y crean una falsa perspectiva.

L'approccio architettonico è istintivo e sperimentale, e si avvale della tecnica della ripetizione, della prospettiva e dell'unità. Lo spazio è modellato a forma di diamante simmetrico con copertura convessa; le pareti sono ad angolo, e contribuiscono a creare una falsa prospettiva con il tetto e il pavimento.

Lotus | Wayne Finschi

Photographer: Shania Shegedyn Chef: Andrew Ballard Address: 172 Toorak Road, South Yarra, Melbourne, Australia Phone: +613 9827 7833 Design concept: Combines a series of objects with lightly earthy forms, soft textures and bright colors.

Lotus is located in Melbourne and its details were worked out by Wayne Finschi, the interior decorator who took charge of the refurbishing project. The result is a combination of eclectic interiors filled with architectural and ornamental touches that conform an enormously attractive theatrical ambience.

Das Lotus liegt in Melbourne, und die Einzelheiten des Lokals stammen von dem Innenarchitekten Wayne Finschi, der die Renovierung betreut hat. Ergebnis seiner Arbeit ist eine Kombination aus vielseitigen Interieurs mit besonderer architektonischer und dekorativer Note, die ein extrem attraktives Theater-Ambiente erzeugen.

Le Lotus est situé à Melbourne. Wayne Finshi, décorateur intérieur, a étudié tous les détails du projet de restauration. Il a ainsi créé un ensemble d'intérieurs éclectiques empreints de touches architecturales et ornementales conférant à l'établissement une ambiance théâtrale des plus agréables.

El Lotus está ubicado en Melbourne. La intervención de Wayne Finschi, interiorista encargado de la rehabilitación de este espacio, ha dado como resultado un establecimiento de interiores eclécticos y plagados de soluciones arquitectónicas y decorativas que componen una atmósfera enormemente teatral y atractiva.

Il Lotus si trova a Melbourne. L'intervento di Wayne Finschi, il decoratore che si è occupato della ristrutturazione di questo spazio, ha dotato il Lotus di una serie di interni eclettici con originali tocchi architettonici e ornamentali, che contribuiscono a creare un'atmosfera teatrale estremamente invitante.

Pelican | Six Degrees Pty Ltd.

Photographer: Shania Shegedyn Chef: Toby Puttock Address: 16 Fitzroy Street, St Kilda, Melbourne, Australia
Phone: +613 9525 5847 Design concept: Unusual structural forms, like the large circular windows visible from
the street make this restaurant stand out from the rest.

From the exterior, oversize circular windows running along the façade represent a powerful visual attraction. These windows frame a half-enclosed area providing access to the premises and act as a bridge between the street and the interior.

Von Außen gesehen bietet die Fassade mit den übergroßen runden Fenstern ein attraktives Bild. Die Fenster rahmen einen halbgeschlossenen Bereich ein und bieten Zugang zu dem Gelände und bilden gleichzeitig einen Übergang zwischen Straße und Innerem.

Depuis l'extérieur, les vastes baies vitrées circulaires sont le point de mire de la façade. Cette surface vitrée encadre une zone semi-couverte permettant un accès facile à l'établissement, à l'instar d'une passerelle entre la rue et l'espace intérieur.

Desde el exterior, generosas aberturas circulares que recorren toda la fachada llaman poderosamente la atención. Estas enormes ventanas enmarcan una zona semicubierta que facilita el acceso al local y hace de puente entre la calle y el interior del café.

Dall'esterno, l'attenzione viene subito richiamata dalle grandi aperture circolari che si rincorrono su tutta la facciata. Queste enormi finestre delimitano un'area semicoperta che facilita l'accesso al locale e collega la strada all'interno del caffè.

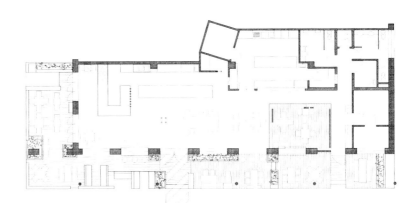

Plan

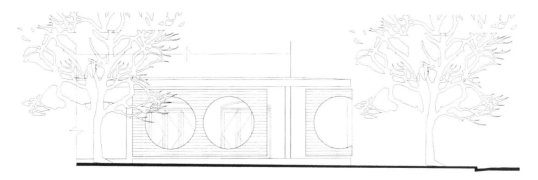

Elevation

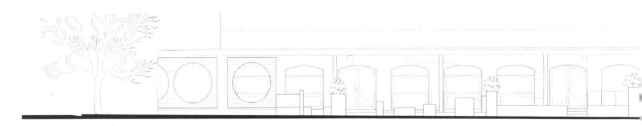

Elevation

Salon Rouge | Grant Amon

Photographer: Shania Shegedyn Chef: Fiona Stark Address: 313 Flinders Lane, Melbourne, Australia Phone: +613 9620 3999 Design concept: The use of color and light are just as important as the choice of furnishings in giving character to this dynamic interior.

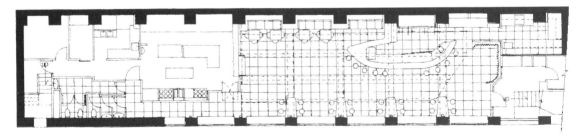

Plan

The particular location and context surrounding the bar have undoubtedly marked its final design. The exterior architecture involves a geometrical front of straight lines with oversized rectangular windows through which a good part of the interior may be viewed.

Die besondere Lage der Bar hat ohne Zweifel großen Einfluss auf ihr endgültiges Design gehabt. Die Außenarchitektur fällt auf durch eine geometrisch entworfene Vorderfront mit geraden Linien und mit übergroßen Fenstern, durch die ein großer Teil des Inneren sichtbar ist.

La situation particulière et le contexte environnant le bar ont un impact évident sur le design final. L'architecture extérieure est constituée d'une façade géométrique linéaire d'où se détachent des fenêtres rectangulaires surdimensionnées laissant transparaître une bonne partie de l'intérieur.

La ubicación y el contexto que rodea el local han marcado irremediablemente su diseño final. En el exterior una fachada plana de líneas geométricas se ve atravesada por enormes ventanales rectangulares desde los que es posible observar perfectamente gran parte del interior del local.

L'ubicazione e il contesto particolari del locale ne hanno influenzato prepotentemente il progetto finale. Dall'esterno, una facciata geometrica dalle linee dritte è dotata di immense finestre rettangolari che consentono di vedere gran parte dell'interno del locale.

Longitudinal section

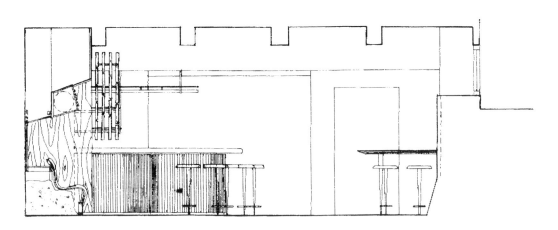

Section

Cruise Bar & Restaurant | Landini Associates

Collaborators: St. Hilliers Interiors Photographer: Ross Honeysett Chef: Warren Turnbull Address: Level 1-2, Overseas Passenger Terminal, West Circular Quay, Sydney, Australia Phone: +612 9251 1188 Design concept: Designer objects and furnishings, and most notably, the restaurant's close relationship with the landscape stand out.

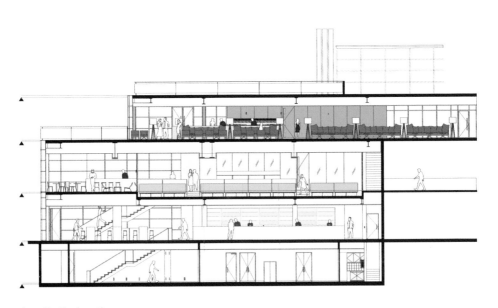

Longitudinal section

A rational and refined architectural style is the backdrop for interiors as attractive as they are functional and modern. The space is organized in different levels, each of which has been granted a specific function. The bar is on the bottom floor, while the upper level contains the restaurant.

Finesse und Rationalismus bilden das Leitmotiv bei der architektonischen Gestaltung dieser Innenräume, die so attraktiv wie funktional und modern sind. Das Lokal ist auf mehreren Ebenen angelegt, wobei jeder Ebene eine andere Funktion zugedacht wurde. Im Untergeschoss befindet sich die Bar, das Obergeschoss beherbergt ein Restaurant.

Une architecture rationelle et dépouillée est la toile de fond de certains intérieurs où se mêlent attrait, fonctionnalité et modernisme. L'espace s'organise autour de différents niveaux dotés d'une fonction spécifique. Le niveau inférieur abrite le bar alors que le restaurant se trouve à l'étage supérieur.

Una arquitectura racionalista y depurada es el telón de fondo de unos interiores tan atractivos como funcionales y modernos. El espacio se ha organizado en diferentes niveles y cada uno de ellos se ha destinado a una función. El inferior acoge el bar, y en el superior se ha ubicado el restaurante.

Una architettura razionalista e essenziale è il punto di riferimento per gli interni di questo locale, che sono allo stesso tempo confortevoli, funzionali e moderni. Lo spazio è suddiviso su più livelli, ognuno dei quali con una funzione specifica. Il bar è sul piano inferiore, mentre quello superiore è riservato al ristorante.

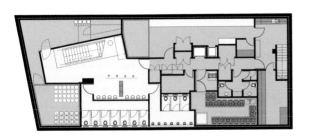

Ground floor

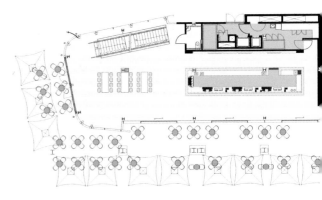

First floor

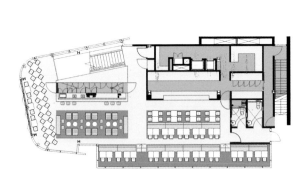

Second floor

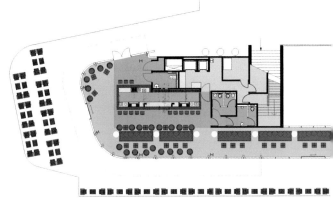

Third floor

Guillaume at
Bennelong Restaurant | Dale Jones-Evans

Photographer: Paul Gosney Chef: Guillaume Brahimi Address: Sydney Opera House, Bennelong Point, Sydney, Australia Phone: +612 9241 1999 Design concept: Ethnic references became the basis for the design of this restaurant in Sydney's famous Opera House.

This restaurant designed by architect Dale Jones-Evans is one of the most prestigious in Sydney. Indigenous, primitive brushstrokes on lamps created by artist Barbra Weir and the flower arrangements, as well as on the diverse pieces distributed throughout stand out in this impeccably designed space.

Dieses Restaurant, ein Projekt des Architekten Dale Jones-Evans, ist eines der berühmtesten Speiselokale von ganz Sydney. Naive und primitive Malereien schmücken die Lampen, deren Entwürfe aus der Hand der Künstlerin Barbara Weir stammen. Auch die Blumengestecke sowie verschiedene Kunstwerke tragen zum erlesenen Stil des eleganten Lokals bei.

Le restaurant conçu par l'architecte Dale Jones-Evans est un des plus prestigieux de Sydney. Les touches indigènes et primitives qui émanent des lampes de l'artiste Barbara Weir, des arrangements floraux ou des divers objets de décoration ressortent dans cet espace au design parfait.

Este restaurante, proyectado por el arquitecto Dale Jones-Evans, goza de gran prestigio en Sydney. Pinceladas originarias y primitivas que se materializan en las lámparas creadas por la artista Barbara Weir, en los centros florales o en diversas piezas de decoración destacan dentro de este espacio impecablemente diseñado.

Questo ristorante progettato dall'architetto Dale Jones-Evans è uno dei più prestigiosi di Sydney. Il tocco primitivo delle lampade create dall'artista Barbra Weir, i decori floreali e i particolari oggetti distribuiti nell'ambiente acquistano notevole risalto in questo spazio progettato in modo impeccabile.

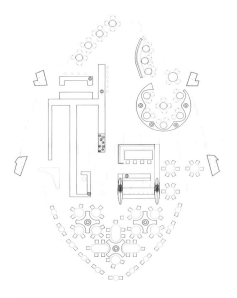

Plan

Dragon-i | India Mahdavi

Collaborators: H. Bourgeois, G. Richard + Arnold Chan (lighting) Photographer: Dragon-i Chef: George Chan
Address: 60 Wyndham Street, Hong Kong, China Phone: +852 3110 1222 Design concept: The repetitive use
of patterns, colors, materials and forms makes for a characteristic and coherent space.

Plan

The decorating of the Dragon-i is based on the fusion of Chinese and Japanese traditions, Oriental mysticism, aesthetic minimalism and beauty. In order to achieve this, a team of designers was hired headed by India Mahdavi, who lives in Paris, with collaborators such as Hervé Bourgeois and Guillaume Richard.

Die Dekoration des Dragon-i ist die Fusion chinesischer und japanischer Tradition, hier mischt sich orientalische Mystik mit Minimalismus fernöstlicher Ästhetik. Zur Realisierung des Projekts zog man so namhafte Künstler wie die in Paris lebende India Mahdavi heran, unter deren Leitung auch Hervé Bourgeois und Guillaume Richard an der Innengestaltung mitarbeiteten.

La décoration du Dragon-i a pris pour thème la fusion des traditions chinoises et japonaises, la mystique orientale, l'esthétique minimaliste et la beauté. Elle a été réalisée par une équipe de designers dirigée par India Mahdavi, résidant à Paris, en collaboration avec Hervé Bourgeois et Guillaume Richard.

La decoración del Dragon-i está basada en la fusión de las tradiciones china y japonesa, la mística oriental, el minimalismo estético y la belleza. Para conseguirlo, se ha contado con un equipo de diseñadores encabezado por India Mahdavi, afincada en París, y con colaboradores como Hervé Bourgeois y Guillaume Richard.

Le decorazioni del Dragon-i si ispirano alle tradizioni Cinesi e Giapponesi, al misticismo, al minimalismo estetico e alla bellezza orientali. Per ottenere questo risultato, è stato reclutato un team di progettisti guidato da India Mahdavi, che vive a Parigi, con collaboratori del calibro di Hervé Bourgeois e Guillaume Richard.

Photographer: Yael Pincus Address: Tel-Aviv Port, Tel-Aviv, Israel Design concept: A combination of contemporary, kitsch and industrial references give character and color to this cutting edge club in Tel-Aviv.

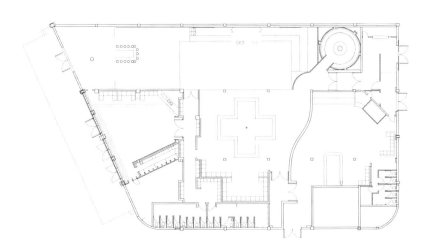

Plan

The design of the club is focused on the creation of good vibrations through the use of color, lights, materials and music. The central area is a wooden dance floor divided in two by a change in floor level, creating two spaces in one.

Good Vibrations stehen im Mittelpunkt des Designs dieses Clubs. Dies wird durch Farbe, Licht, die Baumaterialien und Musik erreicht. Der zentrale Raum ist eine Tanzfläche aus Holz, die durch die Anlage auf zwei leicht unterschiedlichen Ebenen so fast unmerklich in zwei verschiedene Ambiente geteilt ist.

Le design de ce club est centré sur la diffusion de vibrations positives par le biais de couleurs, lumières, matériaux et musiques. L'espace central est une piste de danse en bois qu'un léger décrochement de niveau partage en deux, créant deux espaces en un.

El diseño de este local se ha centrado en la creación de buenas vibraciones a través del color, las luces, los materiales y la música. El área central es una pista de baile con suelo de madera dividido en dos por un ligero desnivel, con lo cual resultan dos espacios en uno.

Il design del locale intende creare delle vibrazioni positive ricorrendo a un uso particolare dei colori, delle luci, dei materiali e della musica. L'area centrale è una pista da ballo in legno divisa in due da un leggero dislivello che crea due spazi in uno.

הודעה
מכירה או עישון
של משקאות חריפים
לעי שבת מלאו לו 18 שנד
אסורה.

J-Pop Odaiba | Katsunori Suzuki/Fantastic Design Works Inc.

Photographers: Nacása & Partners Address: Decks Tokyo Beach, 1-6-1 Daiba, Tokyo, Japan Phone: +81 03 35705767 Design concept: A high-tech aesthetic coupled with colorful, organic forms makes way for an alternative space to the common café.

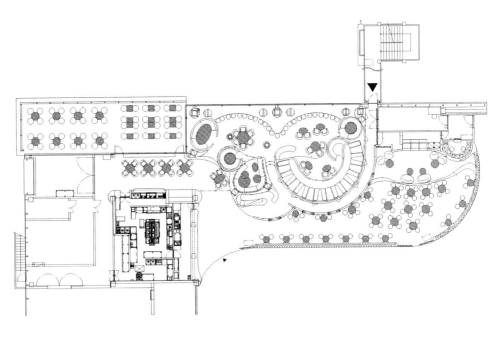

Plan

To counteract the indoor location, Katsunori Suzuki's team based the design on detailed organic shapes whose colors match the constantly changing light. They inspired their design on the roots of a tree trunk in creating the shapes and forms that compose the project.

Um einen Kontrast zum Innenraum zu bilden, ließ sich das Team von Katsunori Suzuki von den verschiedensten organischen Formen inspirieren, deren Farben mit dem konstant wechselnden Licht harmonisieren. Das Design lehnt an die Formen der Wurzeln eines Baumstammes an, deren Umrisse und Formen die Grundelemente dieser Gestaltung bilden.

Pour parer à la situation intérieure, l'équipe de Katsunori Suzuki a basé son design sur des formes organiques dont les couleurs évoluent au gré des changements de lumière constants. En concevant les contours et les formes du projet, ils ont crée un design inspiré de racines d'arbres.

Para contrarrestar la localización interior, el equipo de Katsunori Suzuki se inspiró en las múltiples formas orgánicas que ofrecen una multitud de tonalidades cambiantes. Las formas que adopta el proyecto están inspiradas en las raíces de árboles y otros elementos vegetales.

Per controbilanciare la collocazione degli interni, l'équipe di Katsunori Suzuki si è ispirata alle molteplici forme organiche che offrono una moltitudine di tonalità cangianti; per creare le forme che compongono l'ambiente, i progettisti hanno tratto ispirazione dalle radici degli alberi e da altri elementi vegetali.

Moph | Claudio Colucci Design

Photographers: Nacása & Partners Chef: Hakka Group Address: 15-1 Udagawa Shibuya, Tokyo, Japan Phone: +81 03 54568244 Design concept: Translucent materials, reflective surfaces and a pop aesthetic are the main ingredients in this original tapas bar.

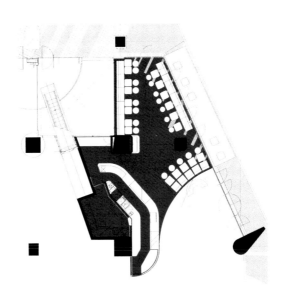

Plan

Twenty-first-century Japan is a mix of cultures in which old Asian traditions are making way for new Western styles: Moph exemplifies this trend through the incorporation of a contemporary Japanese aesthetic, Spanish cuisine in the form of tapas and a sprinkling of the Anglo-Saxon.

Das Japan des 21. Jahrhunderts ist eine Mischung der Kulturen, bei der alte japanische Traditionen durch neuen westlichen Stil abgelöst werden. Im Moph wird diese Tendenz ganz besonders deutlich, denn hier mischt sich zeitgenössische japanische Ästhetik mit spanischen Tapas und einem Touch angelsächsischer Tradition.

Le Japon du 21e siècle est un mélange de cultures où les anciennes traditions de l'Asie s'ouvrent aux nouveaux styles occidentaux : le Moph traduit cette tendance en intégrant l'esthétique contemporaine japonaise, les tapas espagnoles et une pincée de culture anglo-saxonne.

El Japón del siglo XXI es una mezcla de culturas en donde las antiguas tradiciones asiáticas dan paso a nuevos estilos occidentales: el Moph ejemplifica esta tendencia mediante la incorporación de la estética contemporánea japonesa, las tapas españolas y el guiño a la cultura anglosajona.

Il Giappone del XXI secolo è un miscuglio di culture dove le antiche tradizioni asiatiche lasciano spazio a nuovi stili occidentali: il Moph esemplifica questa tendenza incorporando l'estetica contemporanea giapponese, la cucina spagnola con le sue tapas e un pizzico di cultura anglosassone.

Europe

Austria

Horitschon   Weninger

Vienna   Bignet
Dennstedt
Palmenhaus

Belgium

Ghent   Grade

Denmark

Copenhagen   Barstarten
NASA
Supergeil Bar

France

Paris   Bon
Cabaret
Georges
Kong
Nirvana

Germany

Berlin   Dietrich
Lounge 808
Universum Lounge

Iceland

Reikjavik   Pravda

Italy

Florence   Universale

Follonica   L'Arca

Milan   Bar Shu

Rome   Supperclub Roma

Netherlands

Amsterdam   Nomads

Spain

Barcelona   Bestial
Cacao Sampaka
CATA 181
El Japonés
Lupino
Oven
Saltapitas
Shi Bui

Madrid   Larios

Pamplona   Sitio

Tarragona   La Mesie

Switzerland

Geneva   35° Fahrenheit

Morat   Le Restaurant des Familles

Zurich   Restaurant Siemens
Schwarzenbach

United Kingdom

Glasgow   Tinderbox

Leeds   Norman Bar

London   Sketch
The Serpentine Gallery Pavillion

Weninger | Propeller Z

Collaborators: Karl Schemmel (structure), Klaus Pokorny/Equation Lighting Design & Halotech (lighting) Photographer: Pez Hejduk Chefs: Franz & Martina Weninger Address: Florianigasse 11, 7312 Horitschon, Austria Phone: +43 2610 42165 Design concept: A minimal intervention, in a sober language, radically changed the image of this winery.

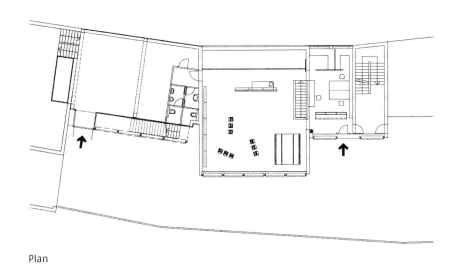

Plan

To improve the services of this old cellar, the space was completely remodeled to include a small gastronomic bar, as well as a store, an office, and a guest bedroom. The building that houses the bodega is a typical farm structure of the region whose functions are grouped in a longitudinal manner.

Um das Serviceangebot dieses alten Weinkellers zu verbessern, wurde das Lokal vollkommen neugestaltet und enthält jetzt eine kleine Bar, in dem auch kleine Speisen angeboten werden, sowie einen Laden, ein Büro und ein Gästeschlafzimmer. Das Gebäude, in dem der Weinkeller untergebracht ist, ist ein typisches Bauernhaus der Region, dessen Wirtschaftsgebäude in Längsrichtung angeordnet sind.

Cette ancienne cave a été entièrement remodelée pour incorporer un petit bar à dégustation, un magasin et une chambre d'hôte. La cave est abritée dans un édifice qui répond à la structure rectangulaire typique des fermes de la région dont les différentes fonctions sont regroupées de manière linéaire.

Esta antigua bodega ha sido reformada para albergar un bar, una tienda, un despacho y una habitación de invitados. La construcción responde a la típica estructura rectangular de granja de la región, donde las funciones se agrupan en forma longitudinal.

Questa antica cantina è stato completamente rimodellata incorporando un piccolo bar gastronomico, un negozio, un ufficio e una stanza per gli ospiti. L'edificio che ospita questo locale mostra la tipica struttura delle cascine di questa regione, dove le diverse attività sono raggruppate in forma longitudinale.

Bignet | René Chavanne

Photographers: Maximilian Kiefhaber, Manfred Seidl & Bignet Chefs: Mr. Goll & Andreas Siller Address: Hoher Markt 8-9, Vienna, Austria Phone: +43 1 533 2939 Design concept: Cushioned seating and well-lit interior make this internet café comfortable and aesthetically pleasing.

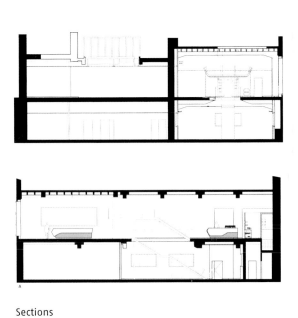

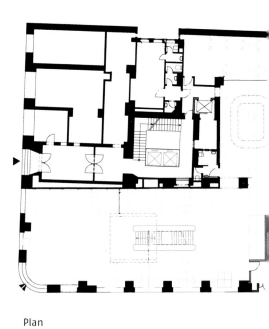

Sections

Plan

Entering this cybercafé entails a whole new experience. The 8,600 square feet that were once the headquarters of a store selling second-hand goods has been transformed at the hands of architect René Chavanne into a large communications center for the twenty-first century.

Schon der Eintritt in dieses Cybercafé ist eine ganz neue Erfahrung. Die 800 m² waren früher Sitz eines Secondhand-Waren-Großhändlers. Der Architekt René Chavanne hat die Räumlichkeiten in ein geräumiges Kommunikationszentrum des 21. Jahrhunderts umgewandelt.

Entrer dans ce cyber café, c'est toute une expérience. L'architecte René Chavanne a transformé les 800 m² de cet ancien dépôt central de marchandises d'occasion en un immense centre de communication adapté au 21e siècle.

Entrar en este cibercafé supone toda una experiencia. Los 800 m² que antaño fueran la sede de una tienda en la que se vendían productos de segunda mano se han transformado de la mano del arquitecto René Chavanne en toda una central de comunicación para el siglo XXI.

Entrare in questo cyber-cafè è un'esperienza totalmente nuova: i suoi 800 m², che una volta ospitavano un negozio di oggetti di seconda mano, sono stati trasformati per mano dell'architetto René Chavanne in un enorme centro di comunicazione del XXI secolo.

Elevation

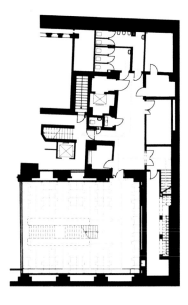

Basement

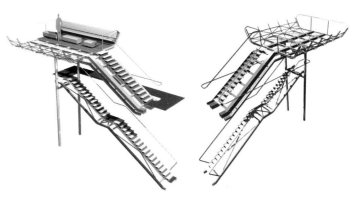

Dennstedt | Werner Larch & Claudia König

Photographer: Margherita Spiluttini Chef: Reinhard Gerers Address: Daungasse 1/Laudongasse 36, Vienna, Austria Phone: +43 1 403 8324 Design concept: Earth tones and natural materials set against a white backdrop generate an elegant and laid-back atmosphere.

Located in a busy area of Vienna, the interiors of this establishment reflect the diversity of the venue, functioning as café, bar, restaurant. The play of light, and the choice materials, textures, and colors define this warm and welcoming avant-garde project.

In einem belebten Viertel von Wien gelegen, reflektiert das Lokal die Vielseitigkeit des Ortes und ist Café, Kneipe und Restaurant in einem. Das Spiel mit Licht und die Wahl von Materialien, Oberflächen und Farben stehen im Vordergrund dieses Avantgarde-Projekts mit warmer und einladender Atmosphäre.

Situé dans une zone très animée de Vienne, cet établissement reflète dans ses intérieurs les diverses utilisations de ses espaces selon les désirs de la clientèle : café, bar et restaurant. Les jeux de lumière et le choix des matériaux, des textures et des couleurs définissent ce projet d'avant-garde, accueillant et chaleureux.

Situado en una concurrida zona de Viena, este establecimiento refleja en sus interiores los diferentes usos que pueden adquirir sus espacios a lo largo del día; puesto que funciona indistintamente como café, bar y restaurante. La iluminación, los materiales, las texturas y los colores definen este espacio cálido y agradable.

Situato in una zona trafficata di Vienna, gli interni di questo edificio riflettono i diversi usi del locale che nel corso della giornata funge da caffè, bar e ristorante. Il gioco di luce e la scelta di materiali, tessuti e colori conferiscono un fascino avanguardistico a questo spazio accogliente.

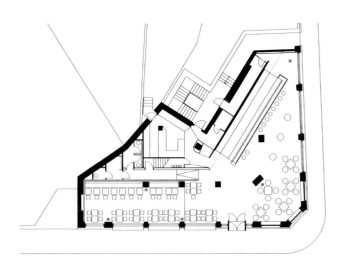

Plan

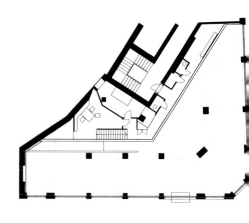

Mezzanine

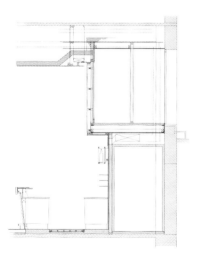

Bar section

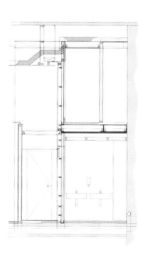

Bathroon section

Palmenhaus

Photographer: Margherita Spiluttini Chef: Mathias Zykan Address: Burggarten 1010, Vienna, Austria Phone: +43 1 533 1033 Design concept: The classical structure was imbued with a contemporary feel through the use of modern furnishings and light fixtures.

The building's central space, which coincides with the highest point, a 15-feet semi-circular ceiling, received a large bar counter that divides the Palmenhaus into a café area and a restaurant area. In fact, the greenhouse feature is played up by the use of palms and other plants as decoration inside the café.

Der Hauptbereich des Gebäudes, der unter dem höchsten Punkt, einer 15 Meter hohen halbrunden Decke liegt, enthält eine lange Theke, die das Palmenhaus in eine Cafeteria-Zone und einen Restaurant-Bereich teilt. Das Gewächshausambiente wird durch den Einsatz von Palmen und anderen Pflanzen im Inneren des Cafés noch unterstrichen.

L'espace central de l'édifice qui coïncide avec le point culminant, un plafond hémisphérique de 15 mètres de haut, accueille un grand comptoir de bar qui divise la Palmeraie en deux zones, un café et un restaurant. En fait, l'aspect de serre est accentué par les palmiers et autres plantes utilisées à l'instar d'éléments décoratifs à l'intérieur du café.

En el espacio central del edificio, que coincide con el punto de mayor altura, un techo semicircular de 15 metros, se ha ubicado la gran barra que reparte el espacio entre el café y el restaurante. El carácter de invernadero queda patente con las palmeras y plantas que alberga el interior del café y que forman parte de su decoración.

Nello spazio centrale dell'edificio, che rappresenta il punto di massima altezza con un tetto semicircolare di 15 metri, è stato collocato il grande bancone del bar che divide lo spazio tra il caffè e il ristorante. Le palme e le altre piante che decorano l'interno del caffè evocano l'immagine di una serra.

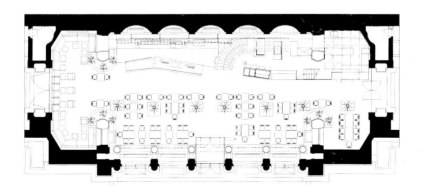

Plan

Grade | Hugo Vanneste

Collaborator: Steven Wittouck Photographer: Bart van Leuven Chef: Piet Rogiers Address: Charles de Kerchovelaan 79-81, Ghent, Belgium Phone: +32 92 24 43 85 Design concept: The Grade presents a mix of visual images and tactile experiences with the aim of stimulating the public's senses.

The Grade bar's design is a combination of contemporary style and nostalgia and complements the restaurant by giving it a light touch of lounge culture. The architect made the most of the space's narrow proportions by conceiving and designing the bar as a free flow of ambiences and impressions.

Das Design der Grade Bar ist eine Mischung aus zeitgenössischem Stil und Nostalgie. Die Bar vervollständigt das Restaurant, indem es ihm eine leichte Lounge-Atmosphäre verleiht. Der Architekt hat den wenigen Platz optimal ausgenutzt und die Bar so gestaltet, dass Ambiente und Impressionen frei fließen können.

Le design du Grade conjugue style contemporain et nostalgie et complète le restaurant en ajoutant une touche de culture « lounge ». L'architecte a optimiser les proportions étriquées de l'espace en dessinant le bar comme un flux continu d'ambiances et d'impressions fluides.

El Grade está diseñado de acuerdo a una combinación de estilo contemporáneo y nostálgico, y lo completa con un ligero toque de cultura "lounge". El arquitecto lo concibió como un fluido de ambientes e impresiones, y trata de sacar el máximo partido a las estrechas proporciones del espacio.

Il design del Grade è una combinazione di stile contemporaneo e di nostalgia, in cui il bar completa il ristorante conferendogli un leggero tocco di cultura "lounge". L'architetto ha concepito ambienti e impressioni estremamente fluidi per ottenere il massimo dalle proporzioni limitate degli spazi.

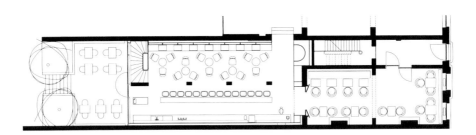

Plan

Barstarten | Finn Andersen

Collaborators: Finn Andersen, Mikkel Max Andersen Photographer: Mads Hansen Address: Kapelvej 1, Copenhagen, Denmark Phone: +45 3524 1100 Design concept: Earth tones and natural materials set against a white backdrop generate an elegant and laid-back atmosphere.

Located in a much frequented part of Copenhagen, this café-bar-restaurant-nightclub displays, in both in its conception and its decoration, the major codes of Scandinavian design: a breath of fresh air in which form is irrevocably marked by function.

Das in einer belebten Gegend Kopenhagens gelegene Lokal, das Café, Kneipe, Restaurant und Nightclub in einem ist, zeigt sowohl in seiner Konzeption als auch in seiner Dekoration die wichtigsten Merkmale skandinavischen Designs: eine frische Brise und eine eindeutig funktionsgeprägte Form.

Situé dans un coin très fréquenté de Copenhague, ce café, bar, restaurant et boîte de nuit affiche, tant par sa conception que dans la décoration, les principaux canons du design scandinave : un souffle d'air frais où forme et fonction ne font qu'un.

Situado en una concurrida zona de Copenhague, este café, bar, restaurante y club nocturno incorpora tanto en su planteamiento como en su decoración las claves del mejor diseño escandinavo: un soplo de aire fresco en el que la forma está irremediablemente marcada por la función.

Questo caffè-bar-ristorante-nightclub situato in una zona molto frequentata di Copenhagen incorpora i maggiori codici del design scandinavo sia nell'architettura che nelle decorazioni: una ventata d'aria fresca in cui la forma è irrimediabilmente legata alla sua funzione.

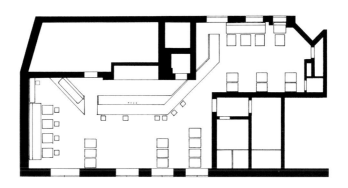

Plan

Photographer: Jens Stoltze Chef: Adam Falbert Address: 8F Gothersgade, Copenhagen, Denmark Phone: +45 3393 7415 Design concept: Futuristic, space-odyssey style interiors characterized by its all-white polished surfaces and custom-designed furnishings.

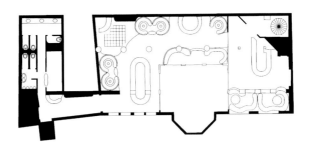

Plan

In order to emphasize the bar's personality, all the details were designed especially for this space, from the ashtrays to the doors. The walls are latex and the floor epoxy; other synthetic materials used are acrylic, fiber glass, Teflon, carbon and plastic.

Um die persönliche Note dieses Lokals zu betonen, wurde hier besonders auf Details Wert gelegt. Vom Aschenbecher bis zu den Türen wurde hier alles speziell für diese Lokalität entworfen: Wände aus Latex, der Boden aus Epoxydharz. Es wurden unterschiedliche synthetische Materialien verwendet. Die Palette reicht von Acryl über Fiberglas und Teflon bis hin zu Karbon und Plastik.

Pour accentuer la personnalité du bar, tous les détails ont été conçus spécialement pour cet espace, du cendrier aux portes. Le murs sont en latex et le sol en résine époxyde. Les autres matériaux synthétiques utilisés sont l'acrylique, la fibre de verre, le téflon, le carbone et le plastique.

Para enfatizar la personalidad del bar, todos los detalles fueron diseñados especialmente, desde los ceniceros hasta las puertas. Las paredes son de látex y el suelo es de epoxy; otros materiales sintéticos utilizados son el acrílico, la fibra de vidrio, el teflón, el carbono y el plástico.

Per enfatizzare la personalità del bar, tutti i dettagli sono stati progettati in funzione dello spazio, dai posacenere alle porte. I muri sono in latex e il pavimento in epoxy; altri materiali sintetici utilizzati sono l'acrilico, la fibra di vetro, il teflon, il carbonio e la plastica.

Supergeil Bar | Johannes Torpe

Photographer: Jens Stoltze Address: Norrebrogade 184, Copenhagen, Denmark Phone: +45 7020 8606 Design concept: The most characteristic element of this bar is undoubtedly its organically undulating wall that adds movement to the space.

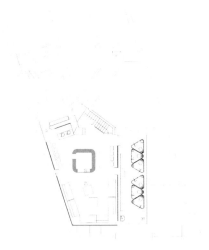

Plans

The walls of the bar are flexible orange units that can change at any given moment to provide a different style of decorating. The flexible material is a new fireproof foam from BASF, and the upholstery is the Danish GUBI Design brand, similar to the fabric used by the old Danish Navy.

Die Wände der Bar bestehen aus flexiblen orangefarbenen Modulen, die jederzeit verändert werden können, und so eine unterschiedliche Aufteilung und so auch Gestaltung des Raumes erlauben. Das hierfür verwendetet Material ist ein feuerfester Schaumstoff der Firma BASF, mit einem Bezug des dänischen Herstellers GUBI Design, angelehnt an die alten Tuchstoffe der dänischen Marine.

Les murs du bar sont des modules flexibles oranges interchangeables à tout moment pour créer un nouveau style de décoration. Le matériau flexible est une nouvelle mousse ignifugée de BASF et les capitonnages sont de la marque danoise GUBI Design, identiques aux tissus utilisés par l'ancienne marine danoise.

Las paredes son flexibles módulos de color naranja que pueden cambiarse en cualquier momento para poder elaborar una decoración diferente. El material empleado en ellos es una nueva espuma antiincendios de BASF, con tapicería de la marca Danish GUBI Design consistente en un viejo tejido de la marina danesa.

Le pareti del bar sono moduli flessibili color arancio che possono cambiare in ogni momento per elaborare un nuovo stile decorativo. Il materiale utilizzato è una nuova schiuma antincendio della BASF, mentre il rivestimento porta il marchio danese GUBI Design riprende un vecchio tessuto usato dalla marina danese.

Bon | Philippe Starck

Photographer: Mihail Moldoveanu Chef: Jean-Marie Amat Address: Rue de la Pompe 25, Paris, France
Phone: +33 1 4072 7000 Design concept: Basic materials and special details mixed with the building's
original elements rescue and refresh the historic value of this colonial house.

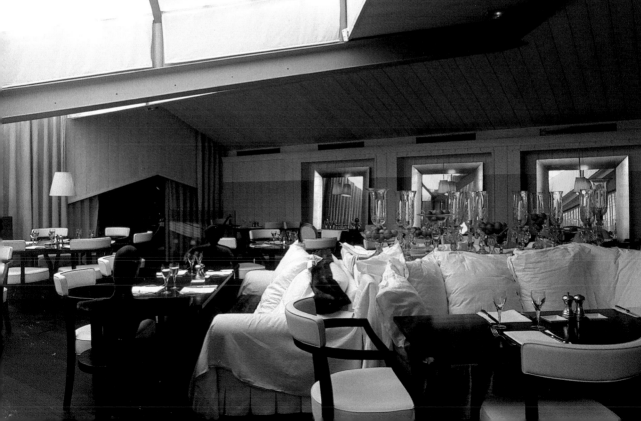

The prestigious designer Philippe Starck was entrusted to transform the interior of this previously abandonded space. The project began with an interesting mix of elements with vast proportions. Thanks to the designer's theatrical flair, the Bon is an ingenious set whose effects form part of the restaurant's spirit.

Der renommierte Designer Philippe Starck war verantwortlich für die Umgestaltung des Interieurs dieser vorher leerstehenden Räumlichkeiten. Das Projekt begann mit einer interessanten Mischung aus Elementen mit ausladenden Proportionen. Dank dem vom Designer geschaffenen besonderen Theaterflair ist aus dem Bon ein origineller Schauplatz geworden, dessen Spezialeffekte einen Teil der Besonderheit des Restaurants ausmachen.

Le prestigieux designer, Philippe Starck, a été chargé de transformer l'espace intérieur de ce lieu abandonné. Le projet à initié un mélange intéressant d'éléments aux proportions importantes. Grâce au talent de mise en scène théâtrale du designer, le Bon est un ensemble où l'ingéniosité des effets façonne l'esprit du restaurant.

El prestigioso diseñador Philippe Starck se encargó de reconvertir este interior a partir de una interesante mezcla de elementos de vastas proporciones. Gracias la teatralidad de este interiorista, el Bon se ha convertido en una especie de decorado donde los efectos se hacen evidentes para formar parte del espíritu del local.

Il famoso designer Philippe Starck si è occupato della riconversione degli interni di questo spazio abbandonato, rimescolando diversi elementi dalle vaste proporzioni. Grazie al gusto teatrale del designer, il Bon è ora un set particolare che esalta lo spirito del ristorante.

Cabaret | Ora-ïto

Photographer: Javier Urquijo/Omnia   Chef: Thierry Gay   Address: Place du Palais Royal 2, Paris, France
Phone: +33 1 5862 5625   Design concept: Ultra-modern design, continuous surfaces and plush lounge furniture for a futuristic effect.

The CAB is a new space inside the Cabaret restaurant that expands the size of this establishment but stays true to the original style. The result is a science-fiction set with aesthetic elements taken from Stanley Kubrick films. The radical architecture is by no means incompatible with rational uses or practicality.

Das CAB ist ein neues Lokal im Inneren des Cabaret-Restaurants. Das bereits existierende Lokal wurde dabei stilgetreu erweitert. Das Resultat ist ein futuristisches Dekor im Stil eines Science-Fiction-Sets aus Filmen von Stanley Kubrick. Trotz radikaler Umsetzung dieses Konzeptes ist das Ergebnis in keiner Weise unvereinbar mit Funktionalität und Nutzbarkeit.

Le CAB est un nouvel espace à l'intérieur du restaurant Cabaret qui l'agrandit tout en restant fidèle au style original. Il en résulte un décor de science fiction doté d'éléments esthétiques tirés des films de Stanley Kubrick. L'architecture extrême n'est en aucun cas incompatible avec la fonctionnalité et la commodité de l'établissement.

El CAB es un nuevo espacio ubicado dentro del restaurante Cabaret que amplía la superficie del local permaneciendo fiel a su decoración. El resultado es un decorado de ciencia ficción con elementos estéticos de las películas de Stanley Kubrick. La radical arquitectura no es incompatible con el uso racional de ésta y la funcionalidad del local.

Il CAB è uno spazio nuovo all'interno del ristorante Cabaret che estende le dimensioni di questa costruzione ma rimane fedele allo stile originale. Il risultato somiglia a un set di science-fiction con elementi estetici ispirati ai film di Stanley Kubrick. L'architettura radicale non è per nulla incompatibile con la funzionalità e l'uso razionale del locale.

Georges | Jakob & McFarlane

Collaborator: Brendan MacFarlane   Photographer: Nicolas Borel/Archipress Chef: Jean Philippe Leboeuf
Address: Place Georges Pompidou, Paris, France Phone: +33 1 4478 4799 Design concept: Modulated from
the same structure as the building, organic forms create a suggestive interior landscape.

The comprehensive remodeling of the Georges Pompidou Center in Paris included the addition of a new restaurant on the sixth floor. The project was to establish an open relationship with the exterior within an architectural context as particular as that of the Pompidou center.

Zu der umfassenden Neugestaltung des Centre Georges Pompidou in Paris gehörte die Einrichtung eines neuen Restaurants im sechsten Stock des Gebäudes. Bei dem Projekt kam es darauf an, eine offene Beziehung zum Außenraum und der architektonischen Umgebung einzugehen und dabei besonders das Centre Pompidou selbst zu berücksichtigen.

La restructuration complète du Centre Georges Pompidou à Paris comprend l'installation d'un nouveau restaurant au 6e étage. L'idée du projet était d'établir un lien avec l'extérieur au sein du contexte architectural si particulier qu'est celui du centre Pompidou.

La reforma integral de la que fue objeto el Centro Georges Pompidou de París incluía la instalación de un restaurante en la sexta planta del edificio. Un espacio que debía establecer una relación con el exterior dentro de un contexto arquitectónico de rasgos tan particulares como es este centro Pompidou.

Il rinnovamento integrale del Centro Georges Pompidou a Parigi ha incluso anche l'installazione di un ristorante al sesto piano dell'edificio. Il progetto intende stabilire un dialogo aperto con l'esterno, grazie al contesto architettonico estremamente particolare del centro Pompidou.

Kong | Philippe Starck

Collaborator: Jean-Jacques Ory Photographer: Pep Escoda Chef: Richard Pommies Address: Rue du Pont Neuf 1, Paris, France Phone: +33 1 4039 0900 Design concept: The printed image makes its presence in the form of photographs, floor coverings and furniture upholstery.

The bar's design is a fusion of French and Japanese cultures, the main link being the image of the traditional geisha and that of modern woman. Thus, the traditional and the contemporary blend in this glass construction that uses similarly transparent furniture to play a spatial game.

Das Design dieser Bar ist eine gelungene Fusion aus französischer und japanischer Kultur. Im Zentrum steht die Rolle der traditionellen japanischen Geisha und der modernen Frau von heute. Tradition und Moderne vermischen sich in dieser Glaskonstruktion und schaffen zusammen mit dem ebenfalls transparenten Mobiliar ein interessantes Spiel aus Licht und Raum.

Le design du bar marie les cultures française et japonaise en alliant l'image de la geisha traditionnelle à celle de la femme actuelle. Traditionnel et contemporain s'unissent dans cette construction de verre où le mobilier, également transparent, instaure des jeux d'espace.

El diseño del local fusiona las culturas francesa y japonesa mediante el hilo conductor de la imagen de la tradicional geisha y de la mujer actual; lo tradicional y lo moderno se conjugan en un recipiente acristalado que utiliza mobiliario también transparente para crear un juego de espacios.

Il design del locale coniuga la cultura francese e giapponese seguendo il filo conduttore della geisha tradizionale e della donna moderna. La tradizione e la contemporaneità si mescolano in questa costruzione di vetro con mobili trasparenti per creare un gioco di spazi.

Collaborators: Aude Pichard (mosaic designer), Fata Morgana (furniture designer) Photographer: Olivier de Saint Blanquat Chef: Maurice Guillouët Address: Avenue Marignon 7, Paris, France Phone: +33 1 5389 1891 Design concept: The eclectic mix of styles, cultural references and materials makes for an unusual and heterogenous space.

Jonathan Amar designed this Paris restaurant located in the area near the Champs Elysées. It is characterized by a combination of styles where the architect gives free rein to fantasy while at the same time imbuing the space with considerable refinement.

Jonathan Amar gestaltete dieses Pariser Restaurant, das sich ganz in der Nähe der Champs-Elysées befindet. Eine interessante Stilmischung kombiniert mit gestalterischer Finesse bestimmen das Innendekor, bei dessen Ausgestaltung der Architekt seiner kreativen Schaffenskraft freies Spiel ließ.

Ce restaurant, situé à proximité des Champs Elysées, fut conçu par Jonathan Amar. L'image de marque de l'édifice est un mélange de styles où l'architecte laisse libre cours à l'imagination tout en insufflant à l'espace une subtile élégance.

Situado en las inmediaciones de los Campos Elíseos en París, este restaurante fue concebido por Jonathan Amar, quien se ha encargado de enmarcarlo en un espíritu de combinación de estilos entre la fantasía desenfrenada y el refinamiento.

Situato nelle vicinanze degli Champs Elysées, questo ristorante fu progettato da Jonathan Amar, che ha combinato diversi stili ricorrendo alla fantasia più sfrenata ma anche a una notevole raffinatezza nella gestione dello spazio.

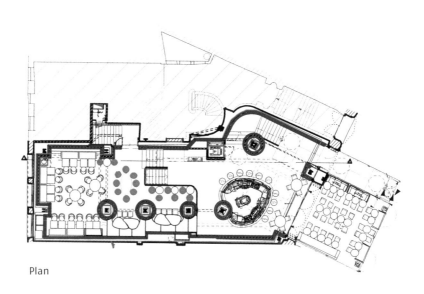

Plan

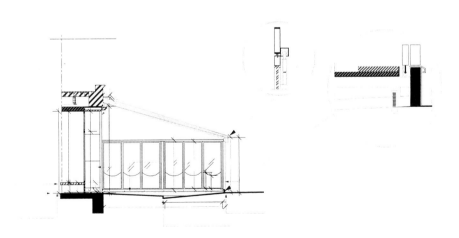

Details

Dietrich | Dani Freixes

Collaborators: Vicente Miranda, Vicenç Bou, Lali González Chef: Anja Unden Photographer: Mihail Moldoveanu
Address: Grand Hyatt Hotel, Potsdamer Platz, Berlin, Germany Design concept: The false wooden ceilings suspended from the roof emphasize the relationship between interior and exterior.

The bar was conceived as the meeting point between the hotel and the street. The architects opted to design a simple plan that meets the basic needs of this type of setting, which is meant to function first as a noodles bar, then as a Russian food restaurant, and finally as a beer hall with fast food.

Die Bar wurde als Treffpunkt zwischen Hotel und Straße konzipiert. Die Architekten entschieden sich für ein einfaches Design, das die Basisanforderungen an diese Art von Umgebung erfüllen, die erst als Nudelbar, dann als russisches Restaurant und zum Schluss als Bierkneipe mit Fast-Food-Angebot funktioniert.

Le bar a été conçu comme un lieu de rencontre entre l'hôtel et la rue. Les architectes ont opté pour un plan simple adaptable aux nécessités de ce genre d'ensemble fait pour fonctionner comme bar à « noodles », puis comme restaurant de cuisine russe et finalement comme brasserie offrant du « fast-food ».

El local se concibió como un punto de encuentro entre el hotel y la calle. Se optó por diseñar un programa que se adaptara a sus necesidades, pensado para que funcionase como un bar de "noodles", después como restaurante de comida rusa y finalmente como cervecería y "fast food".

Il locale è stato concepito come un punto d'incontro tra l'hotel e la strada; gli architetti hanno infatti optato per un progetto semplice che si adattasse a diverse esigenze, fungendo da locale con piatti di pasta, da ristorante con cucina russa e da birreria con "fast food".

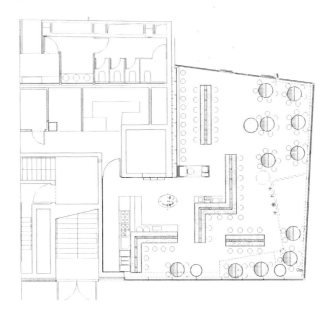

Plan

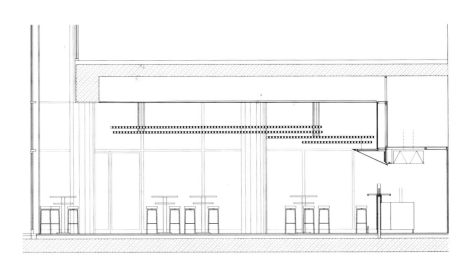

Section

Lounge 808 | Plajer & Franz Studio

Photographer: Fritz Busam Address: Oranienburger Strasse 42-43, Berlin, Germany Phone: +49 30 2804 6727
Design concept: This bar stands out for its unique treatment of materials, geometric shapes and indirect lighting.

At Lounge 808, the designers wanted to offer a place for people looking for a 1950's aesthetic, a place that encouraged guests to come dressed appropriately, to have a cocktail, to hark back to another era in which they would have ordered a dry martini.

Mit der Lounge 808 plante man ein Lokal, das an Ästhetik und Design der 50er Jahre erinnern sollte. Es sollte ein Ort entstehen, für den sich die Gäste dem Anlass entsprechend kleiden, einen Cocktail bestellen, um eine kleine Zeitreise in eine Zeit zu unternehmen, in der man einen Dry Martini bestellt hätte.

Avec le Lounge 808, les designers ont voulu créer un endroit pour les amoureux de l'esthétique des années cinquante et qui incite les hôtes à venir en tenue correcte y prendre un cocktail en s'imaginant être à une autre époque où ils auraient commandé un martini dry.

El Lounge 808 apareció con el deseo de ofrecer un lugar a aquellos que ansiaban un espacio de estética de los cincuenta, que hiciera a la gente vestirse adecuadamente para visitarlo, en donde pudiera tomarse un cóctel y la imaginación viajara a épocas remotas donde tomar un vermú seco.

Al Lunge 808 i progettisti volevano offrire un luogo con un'estetica anni cinquanta, un locale che incoraggiasse a vestirsi in maniera adeguata per gustare un cocktail, dove i clienti potessero viaggiare con l'immaginazione e tornare in un'epoca in cui si sorseggiava martini dry.

Universum Lounge | Plajer & Franz Studio

Photographer: Karl Bongartz Chef: Franco Francucci Address: Kurfürstendamm 153, Berlin, Germany Phone: +49 30 8906 4995 Design concept: Images of space and retro-futuristic forms fill this space adorned by noble materials and linear forms.

Different contemporary versions of Art Déco materials were used to transform a movie theater into a lounge. Brown and white imitation leather stools reinforce this retro feeling of the 60's moonwalk era.

Zeitgenössische Versionen ehemaliger Art-Déco-Elemente wurden für die Umgestaltung des ehemaligen Kinos in eine Lounge verwendet. Weißbraune Barhocker mit Lederimitatpolstern vermitteln einen Hauch von Retro-Gefühl an die Epoche der ersten Mondlandung in den 60er Jahren.

Diverses versions contemporaines de matériaux Art Déco ont été utilisées pour transformer une salle de cinéma en lounge. Des tabourets brun et blanc en imitation cuir accentuent l'ambiance rétro de l'époque des premiers pas sur la lune des années soixante.

Diferentes versiones de materiales Art Déco se emplearon para transformar un cine en un lounge. Taburetes de imitación de cuero en tonos marrones y blancos refuerzan la sensación de viaje lunar de los sesenta.

Diverse versioni contemporanee di materiali Art Déco sono stati utilizzati per trasformare un cinema in una lounge. Le poltrone in finta pelle marrone e bianca ribadiscono la sensazione anni'60 di un viaggio sulla luna.

Pravda | Michael Young

Photographer: Ari Magg Address: Austurstraeti 22, Reikjavik, Iceland Phone: +354 552 9222 Design concept: This place balances traditional, indigenous construction systems with pieces of contemporary furniture designed by prestigious firms.

The designer's main objectives were to create an atmosphere conducive to amusement and to breathe enthusiasm and freshness into all the nightclub's zones. Young relied on Icelandic artisan techniques that he admired, such as the manipulation of concrete and steel in the construction of thermal zones.

Hauptziel des Designers war es, frischen Wind in die bestehende Nachtclub-Szene zu bringen und eine Atmosphäre zu schaffen, die den Gast dazu einlädt, Spaß zu haben. Young griff dabei auf isländische Handwerkstechniken zurück, die er bewunderte, wie beispielsweise die Verwendung von Beton und Stahl beim Bau der Thermalzonen.

Les principaux objectifs du designer étaient de créer une atmosphère propice au divertissement et d'insuffler enthousiasme et fraîcheur à toutes les zones de la boîte de nuit. Young a utilisé les techniques artisanales islandaises dont il est un fervent admirateur, à l'instar de la manipulation du béton et de l'acier dans la construction de zones thermales.

El objetivo principal del diseñador era generar un ambiente propicio para la diversión, de modo que intentó imprimir entusiasmo y frescura a todos los espacios del local. Young se apoyó en técnicas artesanales islandesas, como el uso del hormigón y del acero en la construcción de áreas termales.

L'obiettivo principale del designer era di creare un ambiente divertente che riempisse di entusiasmo e freschezza ogni angolo del locale. Young si è affidato alle tradizionali tecniche artigianali islandesi come la lavorazione dell'acciaio e del calcestruzzo per la costruzione delle aree termali.

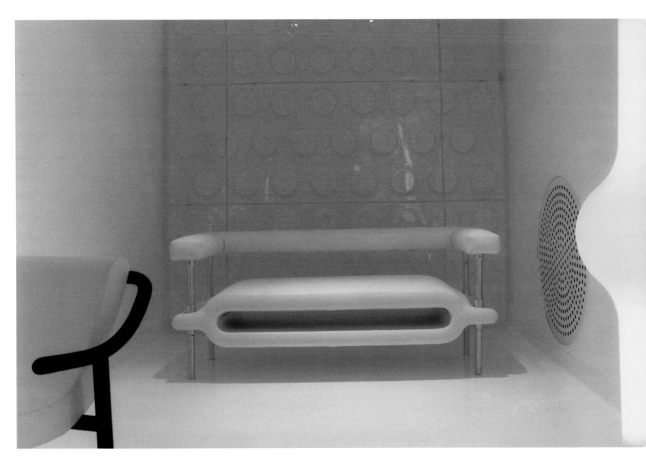

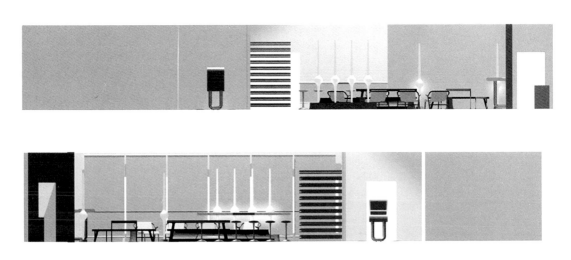

Elevations

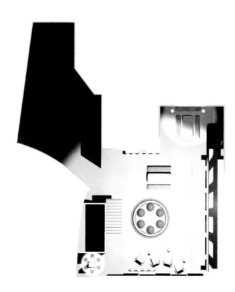

Ground floor

Sections

Universale | Stefano Pirovano

Photographer: Yael Pincus Chef: Giuseppe Ancona Address: Via Pisana 77r, Florence, Italy Phone: +39 055221122 Design concept: Cinematic motifs and theatrical elements transform this bar into a world of fantasy and fun.

The Universale, a multi-use space in the Italian city of Florence, provides this museum-like city with nightlife. Located in an old theater, the Universale does not abandon its past of footlights; the new space is decorated with rich iconography and references to cinema.

Das Universale ist ein multifunktionales Gebäude in Florenz, das für das Nachtleben in dieser leicht musealen Stadt sorgt. Es ist in einem alten Theater untergebracht. Ein bisschen Rampenlicht der Vergangenheit ist noch zu spüren: Zahlreiche Bilder und Darstellungen erinnern an die alten Tage des ehemaligen Kinopalastes.

L'Universale, un espace polyvalent dans la ville italienne de Florence, est le lieu d'activité nocturne de cette ville musée. Situé dans un ancien théâtre, l'Universale n'oublie pas son passé glorieux : la décoration de ce nouvel établissement est placé sous le signe de l'abondance iconographique et des références au cinéma.

El Universale es un multiespacio de la ciudad italiana de Florencia que aporta actividad nocturna a una de las ciudades-museo por antonomasia. Ubicado en un antiguo teatro, el Universale no olvida su pasado de candilejas y decora el nuevo local con iconografía y referencias del cine.

L'Universale è uno spazio multifunzione a Firenze che offre diverse possibilità per la vita notturna di questa città-museo. Situato in un vecchio teatro, l'Universale non rinnega il suo passato artistico e accoglie un nuovo spazio decorato con una ricca iconografia e riferimenti cinematografici.

L'Arca | Antonello Boschi

Photographer: Alessandro Ciampi Address: Via Carducci, Follonica, Italy Phone: +39 0566263639 Design concept: Wood and steel are the main elements used to shape and adorn this floating bar.

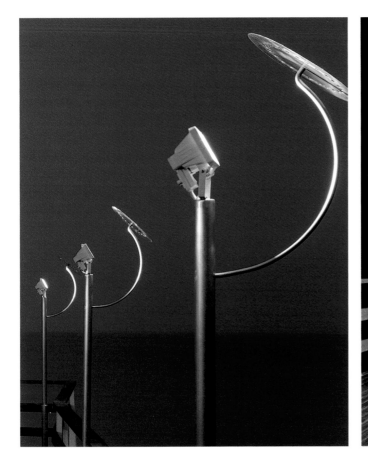

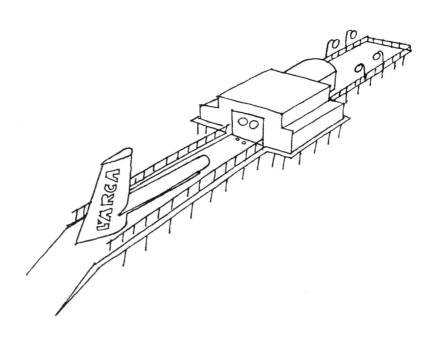

A wooden body with rationalist, geometrical lines quietly penetrates the tranquil crystalline waters of the sea of seas. L'Arca is sits quietly on the old sea, the Mediterranean, cradle of the Latin cultures.

Ein Körper aus Holz mit rationalistischer, geometrischer Linienführung durchbricht die stillen, kristallklaren Wasser des Meeres aller Meere. L'Arca liegt an einem ruhigen Platz am Mittelmeer, Wiege unserer abendländischen Kultur.

Un corps de bois aux lignes géométriques épurées pénètre calmement les eaux tranquilles et cristallines de la mer des mers. L'Arca repose doucement sur la mer de l'Antiquité, la Méditerranée, berceau des cultures latines.

Un cuerpo de madera de líneas racionalistas y geométricas penetra sin estridencias en las tranquilas y cristalinas aguas del mar de los mares. L'Arca reposa sosegada sobre el mar antiguo, cuna de las culturas latinas: el Mediterráneo.

Un corpo di legno con linee razionaliste e geometriche penetra le acque tranquille e cristalline del mare dei mari. L'Arca riposa proprio sull'antico mare, culla della cultura latina: il Mediterraneo.

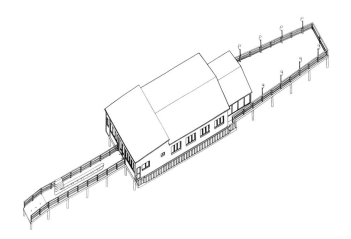

Axonometry

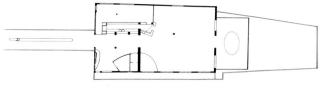

Plan

Bar Shu | Fabio Novembre

Collaborators: Marco Braga, Lorenzo De Nicola Photographer: Alberto Ferrero Chef: Marie Gazmir + Alberto HG. Ramírez Address: Molino delle Armi Streey, Milan, Italy Phone: +39 0258315720 Design concept: Egyptian mythology and the most avant-garde trends inspire this restaurant in Milan, which merges reality and fiction.

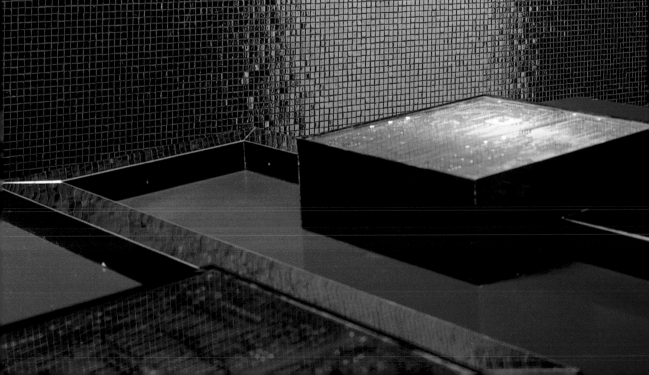

The Italian architect Fabio Novembre designed this project, which is distinguished by its theatrical and eclectic spirit. The original mixture of trends, stirs the imagination and delights the senses of all who visit this fashionable setting in Milan.

Der italienische Architekt Fabio Novembre zeichnet für dieses Projekt verantwortlich, das durch seine besondere, stimmungsvolle Ausstrahlung überzeugt. Die originelle Trendmischung dieses Mailänder In-Lokals regt die Phantasie an und ist ein wahres Fest für die Sinne.

L'architecte italien Fabio Novembre a dessiné ce projet qui se distingue par son esprit à la fois théâtrale et éclectique. Le mélange original de tendances, éveille l'imagination et ravit les sens de tous ceux qui visitent cet établissement milanais à la mode.

El arquitecto italiano Fabio Novembre diseñó este proyecto, que destaca por su carácter teatral y espíritu ecléctico. La original mezcla de estilos provoca la imaginación y despierta los sentidos de quienes visitan este local de moda en Milán.

L'architetto italiano Fabio Novembre ha ideato questo progetto con un carattere teatrale e spirito eclettico, ottenendo un miscuglio originale di tendenze; non a caso, questo locale di moda a Milano solletica l'immaginazione e soddisfa appieno i sensi dei suoi avventori.

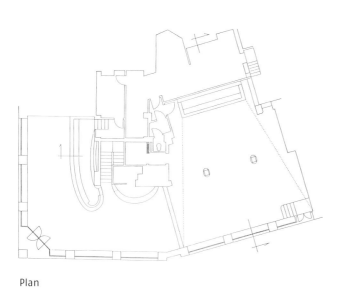

Plan

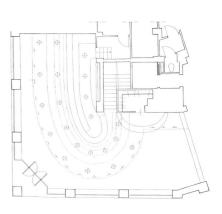

Bar detail

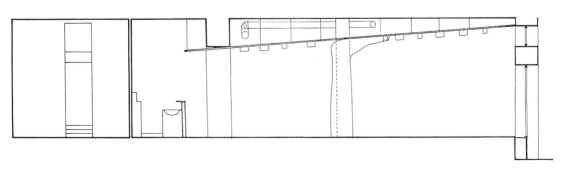

Section

Supperclub Roma | Concrete Architectural Associates

Photographers: Concrete Architectural Associates   Address: Via de Nari 14, Rome, Italy   Phone: +39 068807207 Design concept: This location is famous for its minimal design and its integration of beds into the chill-out bar concept.

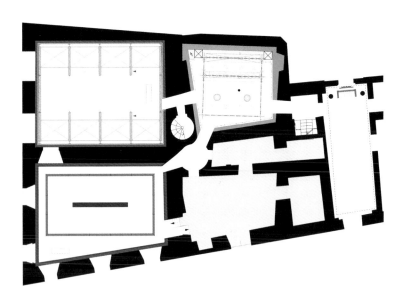

Plan

The Supperclub Roma is located in an old convent, very close to the Roman Pantheon, in the old part of the city. The restoration attempted to recapture the original form of the monument, and now hosts a club and a restaurant; in the latter everything was completely rebuilt.

Der Supperclub Roma liegt in einem ehemaligen Kloster nahe dem Pantheon in der Altstadt von Rom. Bei den Restaurationsarbeiten des Gebäudes war die Zentralidee, das historische Gebäude in seiner Originalform zu erhalten. Heute beherbergt das Gebäude einen Club und ein Restaurant. Vor kurzem wurden beide komplett renoviert.

Le Supperclub Roma est situé dans un ancien couvent, dans la vieille ville, tout près du Panthéon romain. Les travaux de restauration ont essayé de redonner au monument sa forme originale qui, aujourd'hui, accueille un club et un restaurant qui a été entièrement reconstruit.

El Supperclub Roma se encuentra ubicado en un antiguo convento, muy cercano al panteón romano, en la parte antigua de la ciudad. El trabajo de restauración del edificio intentó rescatar el monumento en su forma original. En la actualidad, alberga un club y un restaurante, este último completamente reconstruido.

Il Supperclub Roma è situato in un vecchio convento molto vicino al Pantheon, nella parte antica della città. Il restauro ha recuperato la forma originale del monumento, che attualmente ospita un club e un ristorante, quest'ultimo completamente ricostruito.

Nomads | Concrete Architectural Associates

Photographer: Concrete Architectural Associates Chefs: Ali Ballout + Bas Copraÿ Address: Rozengracht 133, Amsterdam, Netherlands Phone: +31 203446401 Design concept: Mystical lighting and exotic fabrics and lampshades complete the chill-out mood of this lay-down bar in Amsterdam.

Section

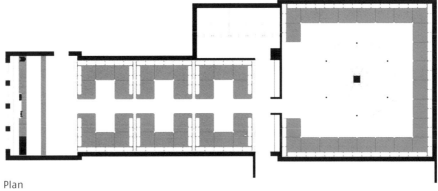

Plan

The building where Nomads is located has been renovated in order to house offices and nightclubs. In Nomads, different types of lighting are used in the design. In the restaurant, handmade Moroccan lampshades provide a diffuse, mystical lighting.

Das Gebäude, in dem sich das Restaurant Nomads befindet, ist seit seiner Renovierung ein Gebäudekomplex für Büros und Nachtclubs. Im Nomads werden bei der Beleuchtung des Raums unterschiedliche Elemente eingesetzt. Handgemachte marokkanische Lampenschirme beleuchten das Restaurant und sorgen für ein mystisches Dämmerlicht.

L'édifice où se trouve le Nomads a été restauré pour abriter des bureaux et des boîtes de nuits. Dans sa conception, le design utilise des sources de lumière différentes. Dans les divers espaces du restaurant, des abat jours marocains, faits à la main, diffusent une lumière mystique tamisée.

El edificio que ocupa el Nomads es una construcción renovada para albergar oficinas y bares nocturnos. En el diseño se han utilizado variados juegos de luces. En los diferentes apartados del restaurante se instalaron portalámparas marroquíes elaborados a mano que crean una iluminación difusa y mística.

L'edificio dove è situato il Nomads è stato ristrutturato per ospitare uffici e locali notturni. Nel design sono stati previsti diversi tipi di illuminazione; infatti, i paralumi marocchini fatti a mano collocati nel ristorante creano una luce diffusa, quasi mistica.

Bestial | Sandra Tarruella and Isabel López. Bet Figueras

Collaborators: Raquel Cabrera, Antoine Baertschi, Frederic Amat (painter) Photographer: Roger Casas Chef: Samuel J. Galdón Address: Ramon Trias Fargas 2-4, Barcelona, Spain Phone: +34 932 240 407 Design concept: An expansive wooden deck terrace takes advantage of the light and views of the Mediterranean landscape.

This Barcelona restaurant is situated in an ample bright space next the Arts Hotel and the Frank O. Gehry sculpture "Peix Daurat". Sandra Tarruella and Isabel López collaborated on a project whose primary objective was to enhance the relation of the restaurant with the beach and the sea.

Dieses Restaurant befindet sich auf dem lichtdurchfluteten ausgedehnten Gelände vor dem Hotel Arts neben der Skulptur „Peix Daurat" von Frank O. Gehry in Barcelona. Sandra Tarruella und Isabel López arbeiteten mit an diesem Projekt, dessen erstes und wichtigstes Vorhaben war, Meer, Strand und Restaurant in einem Kontext zu verbinden.

Ce restaurant se situe à Barcelone, dans un grand espace lumineux, à côté de l'hôtel des Arts et de la sculpture « Peix Daurat » de Frank O. Gehry. Ce projet est issu de la collaboration ente Sandra Tarruella et Isabel López avec pour objectif essentiel la mise en valeur de la relation entre le restaurant, la plage et la mer.

Este restaurante se sitúa en un amplio y luminoso espacio junto al hotel Arts y a la escultura "Peix Daurat" de Frank O. Gehry, en Barcelona. Sandra Tarruella e Isabel López intervinieron con un proyecto cuyo objetivo primordial era potenciar la relación del restaurante con la playa y el mar.

Questo ristorante di Barcellona è situato in uno spazio ampio e luminoso vicino all'hotel Arts e alla scultura "Peix Daurat" di Frank O. Gehry. Sandra Tarruella e Isabel López hanno collaborato al progetto con il principale obiettivo di valorizzare il rapporto del ristorante con la spiaggia e il mare.

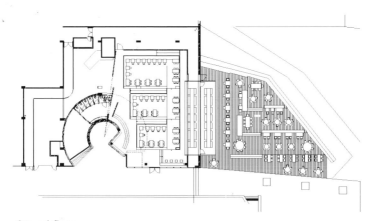

Ground floor

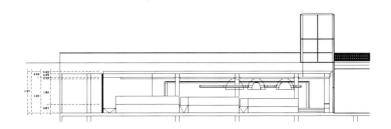

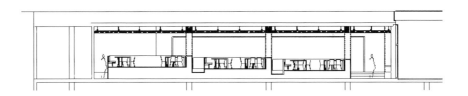

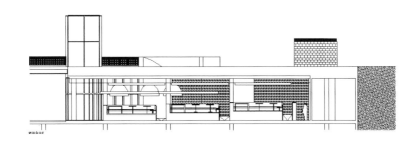

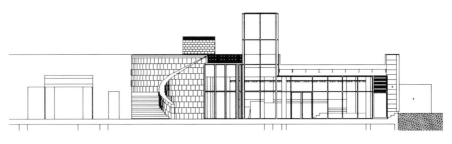

Sections

Cacao Sampaka | Antoni Arola

Collaborators: **Sylvain Calvet, Jordi Tamayo** Photographer: **Eugeni Pons** Address: **Consell de Cent 292, Barcelona, Spain** Phone: **+34 932 720 833** Design concept: **This elongated space offers a succession of spaces dedicated to the exploration of the world of chocolate.**

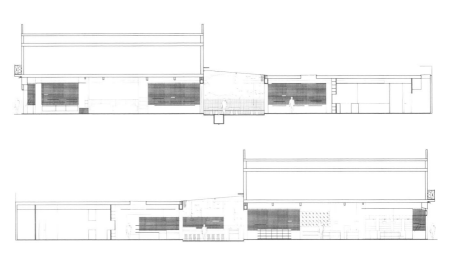

Sections

The space breaks down barriers and visual obstacles through the use of mobile furnishings and an order that allows the public to roam around freely. Aesthetically, this space proposes a setting with refined, exotic and tropical allusions to chocolate.

Begrenzungen und optische Barrieren des Raumes werden von mobilem Mobiliar durchbrochen, das so angeordnet ist, dass die Gäste unbehindert umherwandern können. Die Ästhetik des Ortes schafft eine exotische Atmosphäre mit tropischen Anklängen, bei der Schokolade eine wichtige Rolle spielt.

L'emploi de meubles mobiles et d'un agencement modulable crée un espace sans limites ni obstacles visuels où le client se déplace à sa guise. Sur le plan esthétique, cet univers offre, à l'instar de touches raffinées, exotiques et tropicales, un décor ambiant faisant allusion au chocolat.

Se trata de un espacio sin barreras ni trabas visuales en el que el cliente puede pasear libremente gracias al orden generado y al empleo de enseres movibles. Estéticamente este espacio propone una atmósfera con refinadas alusiones al origen exótico y tropical del chocolate.

Nello spazio, le barriere e gli ostacoli visivi sono annullati da mobili che si possono spostare per consentire alla clientela di muoversi liberamente. Da un punto di vista estetico, l'ambiente allude al cioccolato in modo raffinato, esotico e tropicale.

Plan

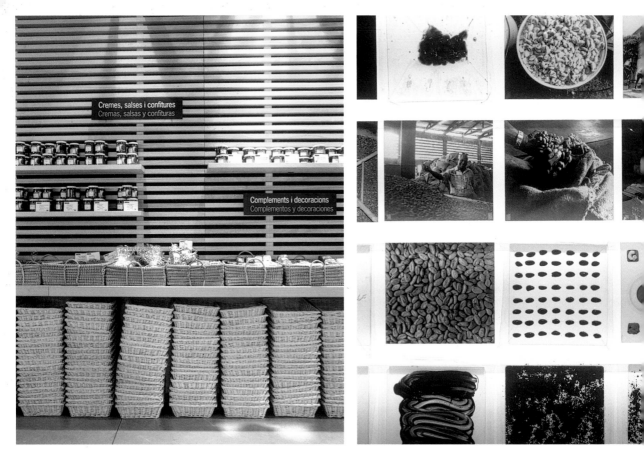

Photographer: Jordi Miralles Chef: Santi Rebes Address: València 181, Barcelona, Spain Phone: +34 933 236 818 Design concept: A predominatly white space highlighted by simple decorative details and diffused light allows the selection of wines to take center stage.

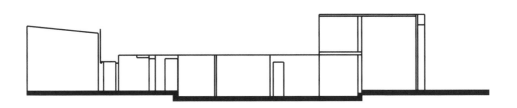

Section

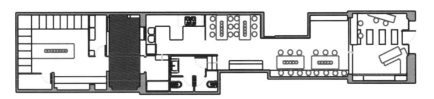

Plan

This bar aims to offer an extensive selection of Spanish and imported wines at reasonable prices with expert advice and suggestions from the sommelier. The wine tasting is accompanied by elegantly presented, original fine dining.

Dieses Lokal bietet eine exzellente Auswahl an spanischen und importierten Weinen, die zu einem guten Preis und mit den anregenden Erklärungen des Sommeliers angeboten werden. Die Weinprobe begleitet ein elegant präsentiertes Menü vorzüglicher Qualität.

Ce bar a pour objectif d'offrir un large éventail de vins espagnols et importés, à bons prix, accompagnés de conseils d'experts et de suggestions du sommelier. La dégustation de vins est agrémentée d'un choix de menus haute cuisine.

El objetivo del local era ofrecer una extensa selección de vinos españoles y de importación, a buen precio, con sugerencias y comentarios especializados del somelier. La degustación de vinos se acompaña con una muy bien presentada selección de platos de alta cocina de autor.

L'obiettivo del locale è quello di offrire una selezione ben fornita di vini spagnoli e esteri a prezzi ragionevoli con i consigli esperti di un sommelier. La degustazione dei vini si accompagna a piatti ricercati di alta cucina.

El Japonés | Sandra Teruella & Isabel López

Collaborators: Emma Masana and Virginia Angulo Photographer: Eugeni Pons Chefs: Manel Silva/Emilio Fernández Address: Passatge de la Concepció 5, Barcelona, Spain Phone: 34 934 872 592 Design concept: The architects manipulated the materials in a forceful language, resulting in a space that interprets the contemporary Japanese aesthetic from a western point of view.

The designers aimed to create an oriental aesthetic reinterpreted for the west. El Japonés interprets the Japanese culture from a personal point of view that includes Japanese films, documentaries, works of art, and modern Japanese architecture.

Den Designern kam es darauf an, eine originelle, für die abendländische Kultur neuerfundene Ästhetik zu schaffen. El Japonés interpretiert die japanische Kultur von einem individuellen Geschichtspunkt aus. Zu auffallenden Merkmalen gehören japanische Spiel- und Dokumentarfilme, Kunstwerke und moderne japanische Architektur.

Les designers ont essayé de créer une esthétique orientale réinterprétée à l'occidentale. El Japonés révèle une interprétation personnelle de la culture japonaise influencée par les films, les documentaires, les œuvres d'art et l'architecture moderne du Japon.

Los diseñadores buscaban una estética oriental reinterpretada desde Occidente. El Japonés evoca reminiscencias a partir de una percepción propia de la cultura japonesa, derivada de la filmografía, obras de arte, arquitectura actual nipona o documentales.

I designers cercavano di ricreare l'estetica orientale e di reinterpretarla per l'occidente. El Japonés rilegge la cultura nipponica in chiave personale influenzata da filmi, documentari e opere d'arte giapponesi, nonché dalla moderna architettura del paese.

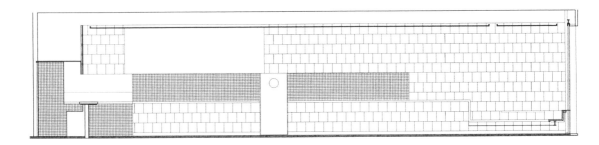

Plan

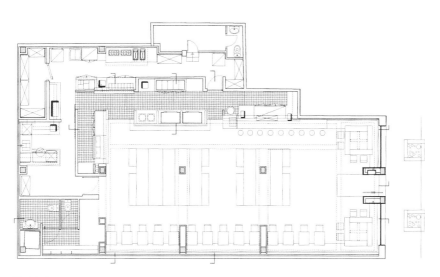

Floor plan

Lupino | Ellen Rapelius and Xavier Franquesa

Collaborator: Miquel Casaponta Photographer: Jordi Miralles Chef: Pol García Address: Carme 33, Barcelona, Spain Phone: +34 934 123 697 Design concept: A clever re-organization of this narrow lot optimized this space to create one of Barcelona's most well-known restaurants.

The shape of the bar makes it look like an airplane because of its narrow width and its 164-foot length that joins the entrances at either end. Despite its small size, the space is used to the fullest: café-lounge, cocktail bar, chill out room, DJ, kitchen, reception and a two-story restaurant and terrace.

Die Form des Lokals erinnert an ein Flugzeug, der schmale Gang und die 50 m Länge verbinden die beiden Eingänge des Lokals. Trotz der extrem reduzierten Grundfläche wurde der Raum optimal genutzt: Es gibt eine Café Lounge, eine Cocktail-Bar, ein Chill-Out, den DJ, eine Küche, die Rezeption sowie ein Restaurant auf zwei Ebenen und eine Terrasse.

Le bar à une forme d'avion liée à l'étroitesse de la largeur et aux 50 m de longueur qui rejoignent les entrées à chaque bout. En dépit de ses dimensions réduites, l'espace est parfaitement utilisé : café-lounge, bar à cocktail, espace chill out, DJ, cuisine, réception et un restaurant à deux étages avec terrasse.

La forma del local se asemeja a un avión por la escasa anchura y por los 50 m de longitud que unen las dos entradas de cada extremo. A pesar de lo reducido del espacio, su aprovechamiento es muy completo: café lounge, bar coctelería, chill out, DJ, cocina, recepción, restaurante a dos niveles y terraza.

La forma del bar lo rende simile a un aeroplano grazie alla pianta stretta e lunga 50 m con due entrate alle estremità. Nonostante le dimensioni ridotte, lo spazio è sfruttato al meglio: café-lounge, cocktail bar, stanza chill out, DJ, cucina, reception, ristorante su due livelli e terrazza.

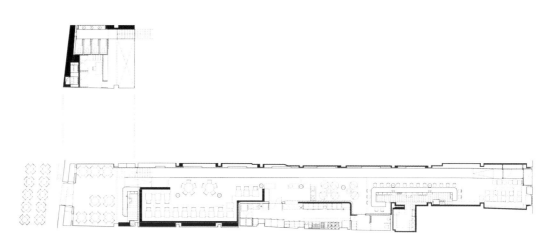

Plan

Oven | 160 BIS Arquitectura + Antoni Arola

Collaborator: Pablo Martín (graphic design) Photographer: Eugeni Pons Chef: Tomás Mora Address: Ramon Turró, Barcelona, Spain Phone: +34 932 210 602 Design concept: The integration of a flexible and multi-purpose venue within a previously industrial warehouse.

This project is an attempt to create a changeable-transformable, multi-use space with its own character. The versatility of the space arises from the industrial and domestic mix and the preservation of the dimensions and materials of the original structure.

Dieses Projekt entstand aus der Idee, einen wandlungsfähigen Innenraum zu gestalten, der zu verschiedenen Zwecken nutzbar sein und dabei gleichzeitig seinen eigenen Charakter haben sollte. Die vielseitige Auslegung des entstandenen Raums wird erreicht durch eine Mischung industrieller Materialien und gewöhnlicher Einrichtungsgegenstände, die unter Berücksichtigung der gegebenen Proportionen und Bausubstanzen dieser ausgebauten Fabrikhalle verwendet wurden.

Ce projet tente de créer un espace modulable à usages multiples et à caractère unique. La polyvalence de l'espace se traduit dans l'alliance entre domestique et industriel, associé au respect des dimensions et des matériaux de la strucutre initiale.

El proyecto parte de una idea que pretendía crear un espacio transformable, de múltiples usos, y a la vez con un carácter propio. La versatilidad del espacio resulta de la mezcla industrial y doméstica y de la preservación de las proporciones y los materiales originales de la nave.

Questo progetto rappresenta il tentativo di creare uno spazio multifunzione altamente trasformabile che possieda un carattere proprio. La versatilità dello spazio nasce dall'incontro di tratti industriali e domestici e dalla conservazione delle dimensioni e dei materiali della struttura originale.

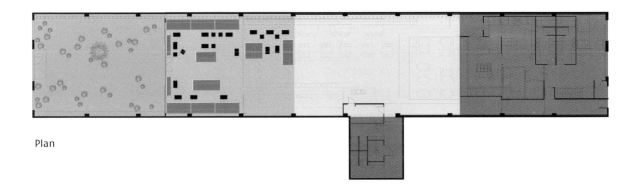

Plan

Saltapitas | Rafael Tamborero, José Luis López

Photographer: Pep Escoda Address: Ribera 10, Barcelona, Spain Phone: +34 933 101 595 Design concept: The combination of unusual materials and and lush textures are complemented by sensual colors and dim lighting.

The colors are pure, intense and warm; tones like fuchsia and orange make for a comfortable, relaxed ambience. The tables, armchairs, bar counters and other furnishings are minimalist and conceptual. It has been recycled elements like columns, windows and the entrance itself.

Die Farben sind rein, intensiv und warm. Farbtöne wie Fuchsia und Orange sorgen für eine angenehme und entspannte Atmosphäre. Tische, Sessel, Theke und andere Möbel sind minimalistisch und konzeptuell. Hier wurden recycelte Elemente wie Säulen, Fenster und der Eingangsbereich verwendet.

Les couleurs sont pures, intenses et chaudes ; les tons, déclinant le fuchsia et l'orange, créent une atmosphère déclinant confort et détente. Tables, fauteuils bars et autres meubles sont d'un design minimaliste et conceptuel. S'utilisent des colonnes, des fenêtres, des vitrages en matières recyclées à l'instar même de l'entrée.

Los colores utilizados son puros, intensos y cálidos; tonos como el fucsia o el naranja ayudan a crear un ambiente cómodo y relajado. Las mesas, los sillones, las barras de bar y el mobiliario son minimalistas y conceptuales. Se han utilizado elementos de reciclaje como columnas, ventanas, cristaleras o la propia entrada.

I colori utilizzati sono puri, intensi e caldi; le tonalità del fucsia e dell'arancio contribuiscono a creare un ambiente accogliente e rilassato. I tavoli, le poltrone, il bancone del bar e gli altri mobili sono in stile minimalista-concettuale. Nel locale sono stati anche collocati elementi riciclati come colonne, finestre, vetrate e l'ingresso stesso.

Shi Bui | Susana Ocaña, Paraservis

Photographer: Eugeni Pons Chef: Ryu-Myung Su Address: Comte d'Urgell 272, Barcelona, Spain Phone: +34 933 219 004 Design concept: As a point of reference in the design of the restaurant, the architects paid heed to the literal translation of the restaurant's name which means "know when to stop".

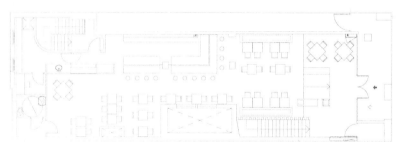

Basement floor

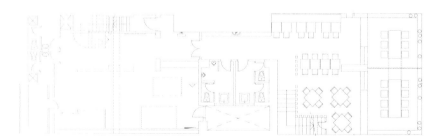

First floor

The Shi Bui was conceived as a cardboard box inside another box. The principal materials —paper and wood—pay tribute to the Japanese culture. A series of quadrangular panels serve as aesthetic screens that hide certain technical installations.

Das Shi Bui wurde als Karton im Inneren eines anderen Kartons entworfen. Die hauptsächlich verwendeten Materialien — Papier und Holz — sind eine Hommage an die japanische Kultur. Mehrere rechteckige Paneele dienen als ästhetische Barrieren, hinter denen Leitungen und Installationen versteckt sind.

Le Shi Bui est conçu comme une boîte en carton insérée dans une autre boîte. Les matériaux de base — papier et bois — rendent hommage à la culture japonaise. Une série de panneaux rectangulaires servent de paravents esthétiques pour dissimuler une partie des installations électriques.

El Shi Bui se concibió como una caja insertada en otra caja. Los materiales protagonistas —el papel y la madera—, son una clara referencia a la cultura nipona. Una serie de paneles cuadrangulares funcionan como pantallas acústicas y ocultan algunas instalaciones técnicas.

Il Shi Bui è stato concepito come una scatola di cartone all'interno di un'altra scatola. I materiali principali — carta e legno — sono un omaggio alla cultura giapponese. Una serie di pannelli quadrati funge da schermi estetici che nascondono alcune installazioni tecniche.

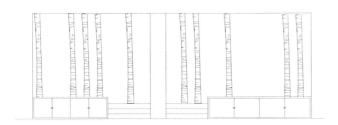

Cross section

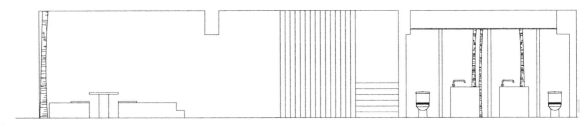

Longitudinal section

Larios | Tomás Alía

Photographer: Ricardo Labougle Address: Silva 4, Madrid, Spain Phone: +34 915 479 394 Design concept: Designer furnishings and lamps create a hip and trendy scene within this café bar in Madrid.

The colorist explosion and creativity of Pop Art, the sobriety of Mies Van der Rohe, the purity of rationalism, the peculiar compositional features of art nouveau, the current vanguard, the industrial style, and aesthetic kitsch inspired the decoration of this bar café.

Die Farbexplosion und Originalität von Pop Art, die Nüchternheit von Mies Van der Rohe, die Reinheit des Rationalismus, die besonderen Funktionen der Art Nouveau, die aktuelle Avantgarde, Industriedesign und ästhetischer Kitsch standen Pate bei der Dekoration dieses Lokals.

L'explosion coloriste et la créativité du Pop Art, la sobriété de Mies Van der Rohe, la pureté du rationalisme, les éléments de composition caractéristiques de l'Art Nouveau, l'Avant-Garde actuelle, le style industriel et le kitsch esthétique ont inspiré la décoration de ce bar café.

La explosión colorista y creativa del pop, la sobriedad de Mies Van der Rohe, la pureza del racionalismo, los peculiares rasgos compositivos del art nouveau, la vanguardia actual, el estilo industrial y la estética kisch sirvieron con inspiración para la decoración de este bar café.

L'esplosione cromatica e creativa della Pop Art, la sobrietà di Mies Van der Rohe, la purezza del razionalismo, le particolari caratteristiche compositive dell'art nouveau, l'avanguardia contemporanea, lo stile industriale e l'estetica kitsch hanno ispirato le decorazioni di questo caffè.

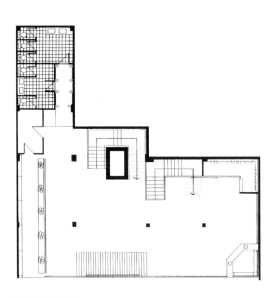

Ground floor

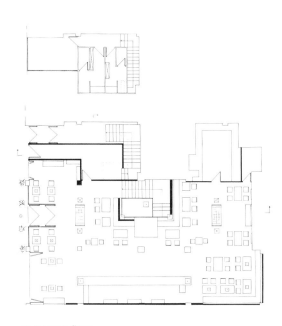

Basement floor

Sitio | Javier Alfaro Bernal

Photographer: Alfonso Perkaz Address: Paulino Caballero 52, Pamplona, Spain Phone: +34 938 235 953
Design concept: A subdue palette of grey tones and the presence of distinctive lighting fixtures.

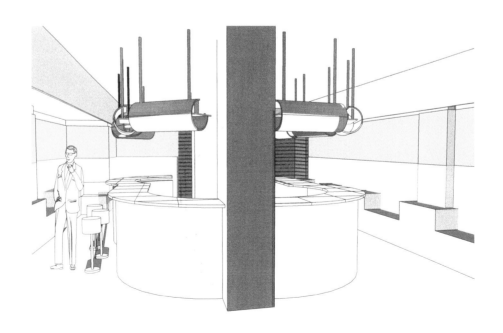

The team organized by architect Javier Alfaro to develop installations for Sitio, on the ground floor of a building in the historical center of Pamplona, conceived the project as one of restoring memorabilia, and recuperation of a classical 60s space.

Das Team unter Leitung des Architekten Javier Alfaro war mit der Entwicklung des Sitio im Erdgeschoss eines Gebäudes im historischen Zentrum von Pamplona beauftragt. Sie gingen dieses Projekt an, indem sie Stücke mit Nostalgiewert restaurierten und stellten auf diese Weise ein klassisches 60er Jahre Lokal wieder her.

L'équipe dirigée par l'architecte Javier Alfaro pour réaliser le Sitio, au rez-de-chaussée d'un édifice du centre historique de Pamplone, a conçu ce projet sous l'angle de la restauration d'un monument historique et de la récupération d'un espace typique des années soixante.

Capitaneado por el arquitecto Javier Alfaro, el equipo responsable de dar forma a Sitio, situado en la planta baja de un edificio del centro histórico pamplonés, concibió este proyecto como la rehabilitación de un lugar con historia propia y la recuperación de un espacio clásico de los años sesenta.

Capitanato dall'architetto Javier Alfano, il gruppo responsabile dello sviluppo del Sitio, al piano terra di un edificio nel centro storico di Pamplona, si è preoccupato di recuperare la storia di questo luogo e di ripristinare un esempio classico di ambientazione anni sessanta.

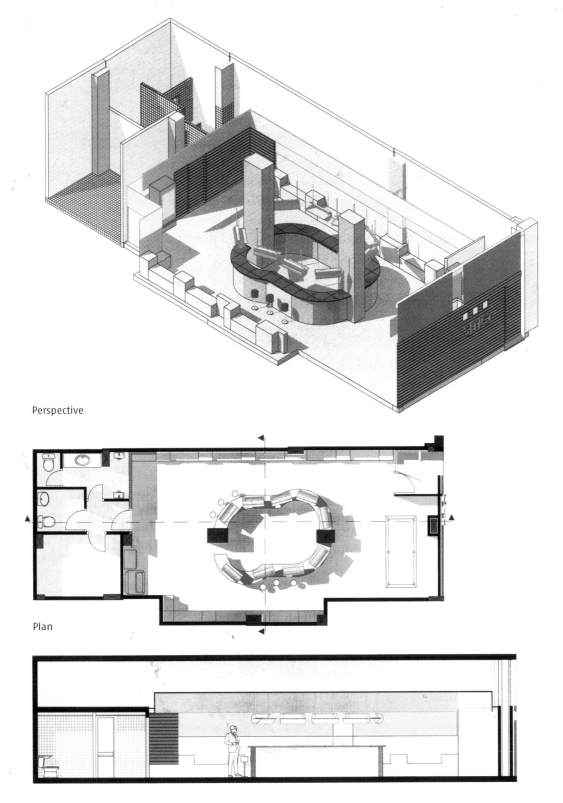

Perspective

Plan

Section

La Mesie | Toni Fàbregas Sisquella

Photographer: Pep Escoda Address: Méndez Núñez 21, Tarragona, Spain Design concept: Projected images on walls serve as the main decorative element in an otherwise bare and simple space.

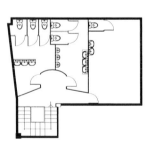

Mezzanine

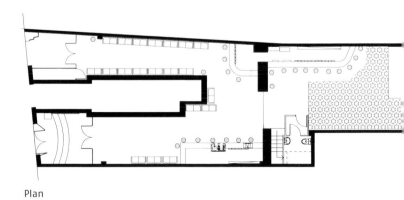

Plan

Most of the ornamental elements in La Mesie are very simple in order to empower the lights the design is based on. These lights, the characteristic feature of the place, allow for a different decorating scheme in each part of the bar.

Ein Großteil der gestalterischen Elemente der Bar La Mesie wurden bewusst schlicht gehalten, um so die Aufmerksamkeit auf die Beleuchtung zu lenken, welche das zentrale Gestaltungsprinzip des Lokals darstellt. Diese charakteristische Ausleuchtung des Lokals bewirkt eine unterschiedliche Wahrnehmung des Raums aus den verschiedenen Ecken der Bar.

La plupart des éléments décoratifs de La Mesie sont simples afin de renforcer le jeu de lumières, concept fondamental du design. Ces lumières, traits caractéristiques du lieu, permettent une décoration différente dans chaque espace du bar au gré des envies.

La mayoría de los elementos ornamentales de La Mesie se proyectaron con gran sencillez para potenciar el juego de luces mediante el cual se consigue crear el diseño del local. Estas luces, que son el rasgo característico, ofrecen la posibilidad de obtener una decoración diferente en cada espacio del bar según se desee.

La maggior parte degli elementi ornamentali de La Mesie sono estremamente semplici per dare risalto alle luci su cui si basa il design del locale. Queste luci, che sono la caratteristica peculiare, consentono di ottenere un diverso schema decorativo in ogni parte del bar.

35° Fahrenheit | Atelier Oï

Photographer: Yves André Address: Rue des Vieux-Grenadiers 10, Geneva, Switzerland Design concept: This industrial space was adorned with the use of color, patterns and retro-futuristic furnishings.

COOL IT

cool IT

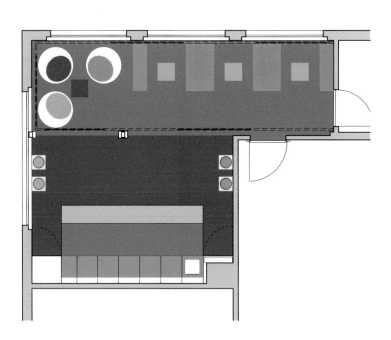

Plan

The futurist design makes the club atemporal: shapes that hark back to the 70's and combine in order to offer a new aesthetic language. Orange and red tones make for a warm atmosphere but are counteracted by cooler greens and whites, balancing out hot and cold.

Das futuristische Design macht diesen Club zeitlos. Formen, die an die der 70er erinnern, wurden kombiniert, um einen neuen ästhetischen Ausdruck zu kreieren. Orangefarbene und rote Farbtöne schaffen eine warme Atmosphäre, die im Kontrast zu den kühleren Farben Grün und Weiß stehen, wodurch ein Gleichgewicht aus heiß und kalt geschaffen wird.

Le design futuriste confère au club son caractère intemporel : formes qui rappellent les années soixante dix et se mélangent pour créer un nouveau langage esthétique. Les tons oranges et rouges engendrent une atmosphère chaleureuse contrecarrée par les blancs et verts, générant ainsi l'équilibre entre le chaud et le froid.

El diseño futurista aporta intemporalidad al local: formas que recrean los sesenta se combinan para ofrecer un nuevo lenguaje estético. Los tonos que generan una cálida atmósfera como los naranjas y rojos se ven contrarrestados por los blancos y verdes, equilibrando lo frío y lo caliente.

Il disegno futurista rende questo locale atemporale: forme che ricreano gli anni settanta si combinano per offrire un nuovo linguaggio estetico. I toni dell'arancio e del rosso contribuiscono a creare un'atmosfera calda, mentre le tonalità del verde e del bianco bilanciano la gamma cromatica con un tocco più freddo.

Collaborators: Desvigne & Dalnoky (landsape architecture), EMCH + Berger AG (civil engineering)
Photographer: Philippe Ruault Address: Morat, Switzerland Design concept: Oxidized metal sheets create a
unique visual intervention in the broad natural landscape.

Out of respect for the natural landscape that surrounds the building, the vegetation of the zone was preserved. The choice of materials, tones and textures, as well as the layout that comprises the installation, serve to accentuate the sensation of a fleeting, perishable structure.

Der gesamte natürliche Baumbestand rund um die Anlage wurde bei der Planung erhalten und das Gebäude fügt sich heute harmonisch in die landschaftliche Umgebung ein. Sowohl die Wahl der Materialien, Farben und Oberflächen wie auch die Gesamtkomposition des Komplexes tragen zum schwerelosen und fast schwebenden Charakter der Anlage bei.

La végétation de la zone a été préservée dans un souci de respect du paysage naturel environnant l'édifice. Le choix des matériaux, des teintes et des textures ainsi que l'agencement des différents espaces configurant l'ensemble, accentuent la sensation de structure éphémère et fugitive.

Se preservó la vegetación de la zona con gran respeto por el paisaje natural que envuelve el edificio. La elección de materiales, tonalidades y texturas así como la disposición de los diferentes espacios que conforman el conjunto se encargan de acentuar la sensación de estructura perecedera y fugaz.

Per rispettare il paesaggio naturale che circonda l'edificio si è mantenuta la vegetazione locale. La scelta di materiali, colori e tessuti e la disposizione dei diversi spazi che costituiscono il complesso contribuiscono ad accentuare la sensazione di una struttura fugace e deperibile.

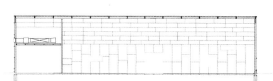

Elevation B-B

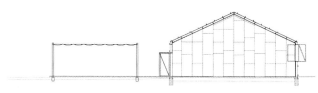

Elevation C-C

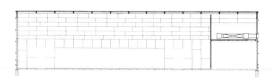

Elevation A-A

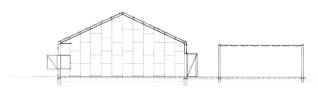

Elevation D-D

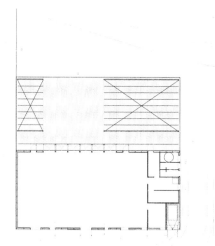

Ground floor

Nord façade

South façade

Restaurant Siemens | Camenzind Gräfensteiner

Photographers: Peter Würmli, Martina Issler Address: Zurich, Switzerland Design concept: The building's relationship with the surrounding landscape is potentiated by the full height windows and exterior terraces.

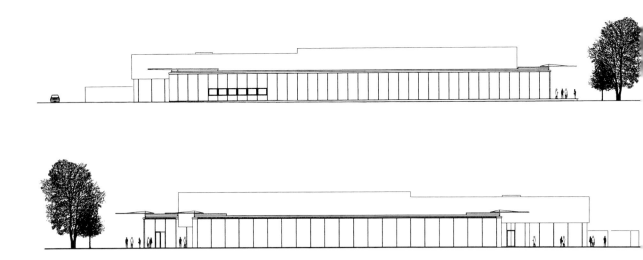

Elevations

This establishment designed by Camenzind Grafensteiner is one of the installations that make up the Siemens headquarters in Zurich. The building houses three restaurants and a cafeteria and has a total capacity of 700. The main restaurant seats 350 and is set up as a self-service restaurant.

Das Gebäude, ein Projekt von Camenzind Grafensteiner, gehört zu der Anlage der Zentralniederlassung der Firma Siemens in Zürich. Im Gebäude befinden sich drei Restaurants und ein Café, mit einer Kapazität für insgesamt 700 Personen. Das Hauptrestaurant, mit Platz für 350 Gäste, ist nach dem Prinzip eines Selbstbedienungsrestaurants gestaltet.

Cet établissement conçu par Camenzind Grafensteiner est une des installations qui fait partie du siège de Siemens à Zurich. L'édifice abrite trois restaurants et une cafétéria avec une capacité d'accueil de 700 personnes. Le restaurant principal dispose de 350 places assises et fonctionne comme un self-service.

Este establecimiento proyectado por Camenzind Grafensteiner forma parte de las instalaciones de la sede central de Siemens en Zurich. El edificio alberga tres restaurantes y una cafetería, con una capacidad total para 700 personas. El restaurante principal cuenta con 350 asientos y funciona como self-service.

Questo insediamento progettato da Camenzind Grafensteiner è parte delle costruzioni che costituiscono il quartier generale della Siemens a Zurigo. L'edificio ospita tre ristoranti e una caffetteria con una capacità totale di 700 persone. Il ristorante principale a self-service conta 350 posti.

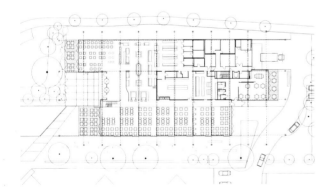

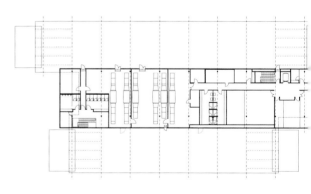

Ground floor

First floor

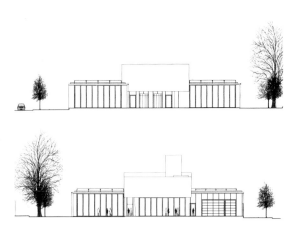

Elevations

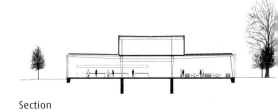

Section

Schwarzenbach | Stefan Zwicky

Photographer: Heinz Unger   Chef: Brigitte Heeb-Schwarzenbach and Hein Schwarzenbach   Address: Münstergasse 17-19, Zurich, Switzerland   Phone: +41 012611315   Design concept: The smooth upholstery and contrast of colors makes this a comfortable and warm space.

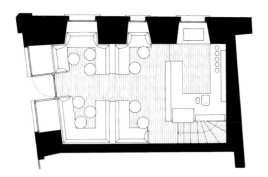

Ground floor

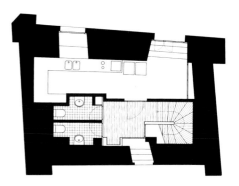

Basement floor

Located in the historical center of the city of Zurich, in a building built in 1662 and modified on several occasions over the years, the Schwarzenbach, founded in 1864, is one of the oldest stores in the city, adding a cafeteria in 1998 to its premises.

Das im historischen Zentrum von Zürich gelegene Gebäude stammt aus dem Jahr 1662 und wurde über die Jahrhunderte mehrfach verändert. Das 1864 gegründete Schwarzenbach ist eines der ältesten Geschäfte der Stadt und verfügt seit 1998 auch über ein Café.

Situé dans le centre historique de Zürich, dans un édifice construit en 1662 et souvent modifié au fil des années, le Schwarzenbach, fondé en 1864, est un des plus anciens magasins de la ville. En 1998, une cafétéria lui a été annexée.

Situado en el centro histórico de Zurich, en un inmueble construido en 1662 que ha sido modificado en varias ocasiones a lo largo de su historia, el Schwarzenbach es una de las tiendas más antiguas de la ciudad, pues data de 1864. En 1998 se anexó una cafetería al local.

Situato nel centro storico di Zurigo, in un edificio del 1662 rimaneggiato in diverse occasioni nel corso degli anni, lo Schwarzenbach è uno dei locali più antichi della città visto che è stato fondato nel 1864, anche se la caffetteria è stata annessa solo nel 1998.

Elevation

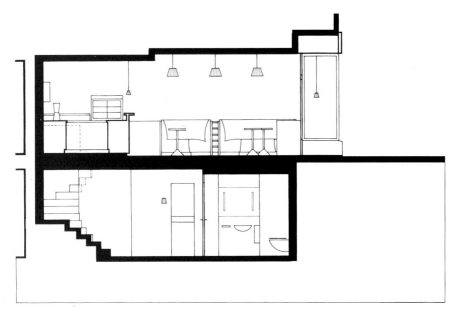

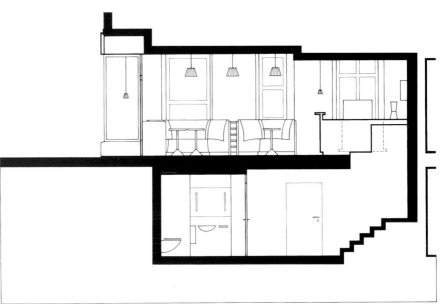

Sections

Tinderbox | Ross Graven

Photographer: Keith Hunter Chef: Gordon Ramsay Address: 189 Byres Rood, Glasgow, UK Phone: +44 0141 339 3108 Design concept: A conservative design that uses noble materials and careful selection of colors to adorn the space.

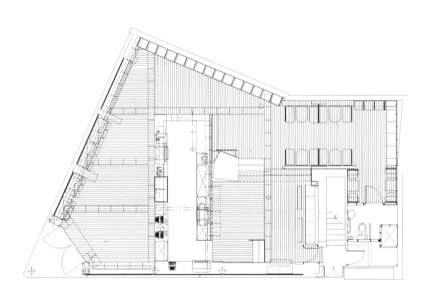

Plan

Architect Ross Graven defined an aesthetically pleasing establishment where the most original proposals would fit without greatly altering the homey-but-functional feel. To fully exploit the potential of the space, different areas are used cater to the needs of the clientele.

Der Architekt Ross Graven entwarf ein ästhetisch ansprechendes Lokal, bei dem auch die ausgefallensten Ideen nichts an der heimeligen und zugleich funktionellen Atmosphäre ändern. Der zur Verfügung stehende Platz wurde optimal ausgenutzt. Es stehen unterschiedliche Bereiche zur Verfügung, um den Wünschen aller Kunden entgegen zu kommen.

L'architecte Ross Graven a conçu un établissement à l'esthétique agréable conjuguant les propositions les plus originales sans négliger le confort et le fonctionnel. Afin d'optimiser l'espace, il a créé différentes zones pour satisfaire les besoins de la clientèle.

El arquitecto Ross Graven se encargó de definir un establecimiento estéticamente atractivo sin olvidar la comodidad y la funcionalidad. A fin de rentabilizar al máximo el espacio, se han creado diferentes áreas destinadas a satisfacer las necesidades particulares de una determinada clientela.

L'architetto Ross Graven si è preoccupato di definire uno spazio esteticamente piacevole senza alterare la sensazione di comodità e funzionalità del luogo. Per sfruttare al massimo le potenzialità dello spazio, diverse aree sono state adibite in modo da soddisfare i bisogni particolari della clientela.

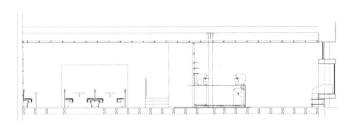

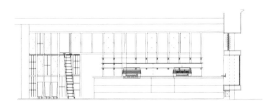

Sections

Norman Bar | JAM (Jamie Anley, Astrid Zala and Matthieu Paillard)

Collaborators: Tom Dixon (furnishings), Inflate (lighting), Fly (graphic design), Tracy Davidson (art)
Photographer: James Winspear Address: 36 Call Lane, Leeds, UK Phone: +44 113 234 3988 Design concept:
combines a series of objects with lightly earthy forms, soft textures, bright colors, and an informal and fun
atmosphere.

The idea behind the Norman was to create a space that combines contemporary design with a warm and active atmosphere. For its design, Tom Dixon specially designed the furnishings, Inflate orchestrated the lighting, Fly controlled the graphics, and Tracy Davidson contributed contemporary art works.

Die ursprüngliche Idee für das Norman bestand darin, einen Ort zu schaffen, an dem sich zeitgenössisches Design mit warmer und aktiver Atmosphäre verbindet. Für das Lokal hat Tom Dixon das Mobiliar entworfen, Inflate die Beleuchtung organisiert, Fly die Graphiken überwacht und Tracy Davidson für die zeitgenössischen Kunstwerke gesorgt.

L'idée derrière la création du Norman était d'allier design contemporain et ambiance chaleureuse et active. Le mobilier, spécialement conçu pour le projet, est l'œuvre de Tom Dixon, l'éclairage porte la marque Infalte, le graphisme est de Fly et les œuvres d'art contemporain sont signées Tracy Davidson.

La idea del Norman buscaba un espacio en el que conjugar el diseño contemporáneo con una atmósfera cálida y activa. El mobiliario, especialmente diseñado para el local, es obra de Tom Dixon; la iluminación llegó de la mano de la firma Inflate; el grafismo, de Fly, y las piezas de arte contemporáneo, de Tracy Davidson.

L'idea alla base del Norman era quella di creare uno spazio che coniugasse il design contemporaneo a un'atmosfera calda e vitale. Il mobilio è stato progettato da Tom Dixon appositamente per il locale; l'illuminazione porta il marchio Inflate, la grafica è di Fly mentre le opere d'arte contemporanea sono creazioni di Tracy Davidson.

Photographer: Ken Hayden/Omnia Chef: Pierre Gagnaire Address: 9 Conduit Street, London, UK Phone: +44 870 777 4488 Design concept: The mixture of stylistic references, high-tech systems and the presence of the artworks make way for a truly heterogeneous space.

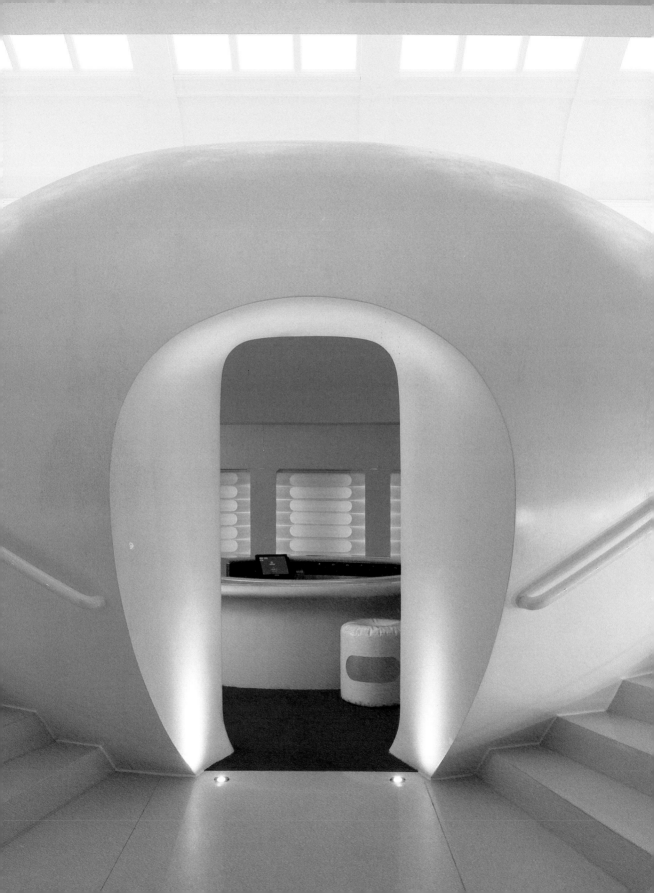

The Sketch is located in an old house in the center of London, very close to Oxford Circus; it has two bars, two restaurants and a bakery. The aesthetic and design of the place was created by many designers of international renown, like Ron Arad and Marc Newson among others.

Das Sketch ist in einer ehemaligen Wohnung im Zentrum von London untergebracht, ganz in der Nähe des Oxford Circus. Das Lokal verfügt über zwei Bars, zwei Restaurants und eine Bäckerei. Ästhetik und Design des Lokals entstanden von Hand verschiedener namhafter internationaler Designer, wie zum Beispiel Ron Arad oder Marc Newson.

Le Sketch est situé dans une vieille maison du centre de Londres, très proche d'Oxford Circus, et il possède deux bars, deux restaurants et une boulangerie. L'esthétique et le design de l'endroit sont l'œuvre de plusieurs designers de renommée internationale, pour ne citer que Ron Arad et Marc Newson.

El Sketch ocupa una antigua vivienda del centro de Londres, muy cerca de Oxford Circus, y cuenta con dos bares, dos restaurantes y una pastelería. La estética y el diseño del local han sido creados por varios diseñadores de gran renombre internacional como Ron Arad o Marc Newson, entre otros.

Lo Sketch si trova in una vecchia casa nel cuore di Londra, vicino a Oxford Circus, e conta due bar, due ristoranti e una panetteria. L'estetica e il design del luogo sono stati ideati da diversi progettisti di fama internazionale, tra cui Ron Arad e Marc Newson.

The Serpentine
Gallery Pavillion | Toyo Ito & Associates Architects

Collaborators: Arup (structures), Robert McAlpine (constructor) Address: Kensington Gardens, London, UK
Design concept: Geometric shapes make way for skylights and windows that filter sunlight into the summer
pavilion and offer framed views of the park.

Serpentine Gallery Pavilion 2002
Toyo Ito with Arup

Capricious forms define the sculptural structure of this seasonal installation, situated during the summer months in the heart of London's Kensington gardens. Designed by Toyo Ito, the construction is a multifunctional space that houses exhibitions, a café and a restaurant.

Kapriziöse Formen bestimmen den skulpturalen Aufbau dieser Anlage im Herzen der Gärten von Kensington, die ausschließlich für die Sommersaison angelegt wurde. Der Entwurf stammt vom Toyo Ito und wurde als multifunktionaler Raum konzipiert, der Veranstaltungen und Ausstellungen Platz bietet und zu dem ein Café und ein Restaurant gehören.

Les formes capricieuses définissent les strucutres sculpturales de cette installation saisonière, située pendant les mois d'été au cœur de Kensington's gardens à Londres. Projetée par Toyo Ito, la construction est conçue comme un espace polyvalent qui abrite évènements, expositions, un café et un restaurant.

Antojadizas formas definen la escultórica estructura de esta instalación veraniega situada en el corazón de los jardines londinenses de Kensington. Proyectada por Toyo Ito, la construcción está concebida como un espacio multifuncional que alberga exposiciones, un café y un restaurante.

Le forme capricciose di questa installazione stagionale, collocata nei mesi estivi ai giardini di Kensington nel cuore di Londra, le conferiscono una struttura scultorea. La costruzione, progettata dall'architetto Toyo Ito, è uno spazio multifunzionale che ospita mostre oltre ad un caffè e a un ristorante.

Plan

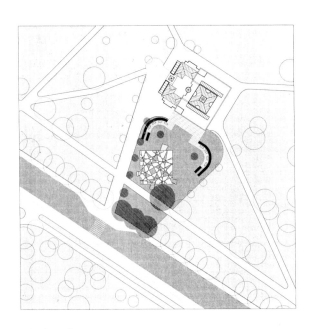

Location plan

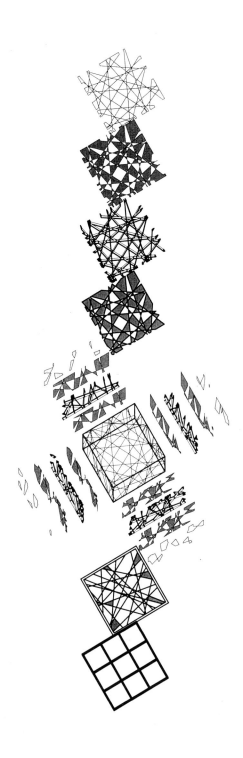